JACK
KIRBY

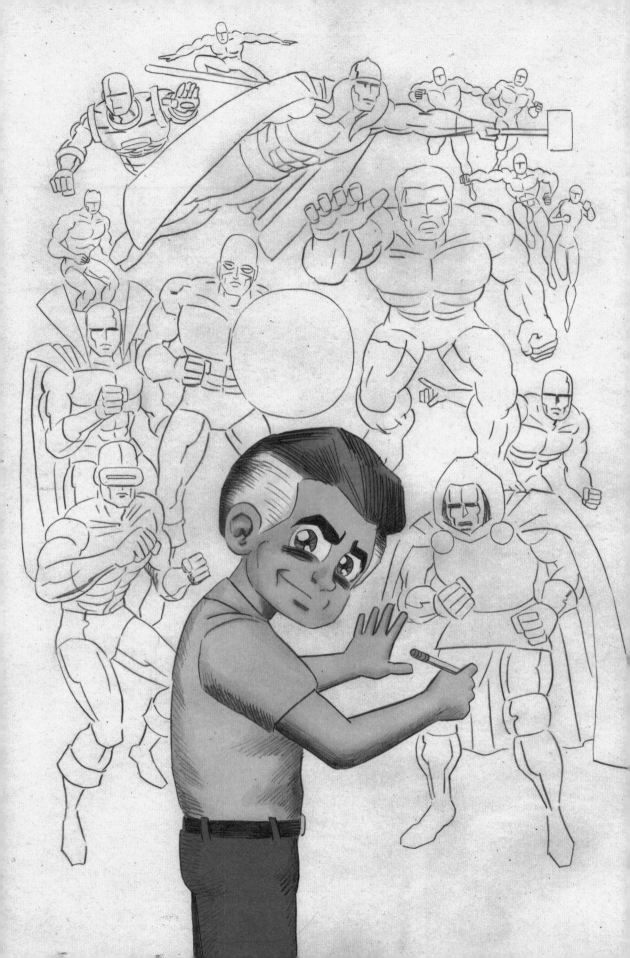

JACK KIRBY

THE EPIC LIFE OF THE
KING OF COMICS

TOM SCIOLI

TEN SPEED PRESS
California | New York

AUTHOR'S NOTE

This is a biography of Jack Kirby, not an autobiography or memoir. The first-person narration in this work is a literary device. The story is told through "Kirby's" point-of-view, adapted from a number of sources, including interviews he gave throughout his life. There are differences of opinion and other points of view about the events depicted in this work.

This book is not authorized by the Jack Kirby Estate, Marvel Entertainment, or DC Comics.

MY FOLKS WERE FROM A PART OF THE AUSTRO-HUNGARIAN EMPIRE CALLED GALICIA. IT WAS A CENTER OF CULTURE AND A HAVEN FOR REFUGEES FROM THE RUSSIAN POGROMS. IT WAS JUST BEFORE GALICIA WAS ENGULFED IN THE FIRST WORLD WAR, AND BEFORE IT WAS WASHED AWAY FOR ALL TIME BY THE HOLOCAUST.

MY MOTHER, ROSE BERNSTEIN, LEFT AS A CHILD AND CAME TO AMERICA WITH HER SISTERS.

MY FATHER, BEN KURTZBERG, WAS FROM A WELL-TO-DO FAMILY. HE OFFENDED A LOCAL DUKE AND GOT CHALLENGED TO A DUEL: SWORDS OR PISTOLS AT DAWN. AT LEAST THAT'S WHAT HE TOLD ME.

HIS FATHER TOLD HIM TO GET OUT OF THE COUNTRY AND GAVE HIM A GOOD BIT OF MONEY TO GET STARTED IN HIS NEW LIFE.

A DOLLAR WENT A LOT FURTHER IN THOSE DAYS, BUT THE MONEY EVENTUALLY RAN OUT AND MY FATHER HAD TO START EARNING.

MY PARENTS MET THROUGH THE AUSTRIAN COMMUNITY IN THE NEIGHBORHOOD. A MATCHMAKER PUT THEM TOGETHER.

BEFORE LONG, THEY WERE MARRIED AND LIVING AT 147 ESSEX STREET ON THE LOWER EAST SIDE.

MY FATHER HAD A JOB IN THE SHMATA INDUSTRY. I GUESS YOU COULD CALL THE PLACE HE WORKED IN A SWEATSHOP.

MY MOTHER WORKED THERE FOR A TIME, TOO.

THEN, ALONG CAME ME, BABY JACOB, BORN AUGUST 28, 1917.

OUR APARTMENT WAS SMALL, BUT MY MOTHER KEPT THE PLACE IMMACULATE.

WHEN I WAS FOUR YEARS OLD, MY LITTLE BROTHER DAVID WAS BORN AT HOME ON THE KITCHEN TABLE.

I WANTED TO BE THERE FOR HIS ARRIVAL, BUT MY FOLKS SENT ME TO STAY WITH THE NEIGHBORS.

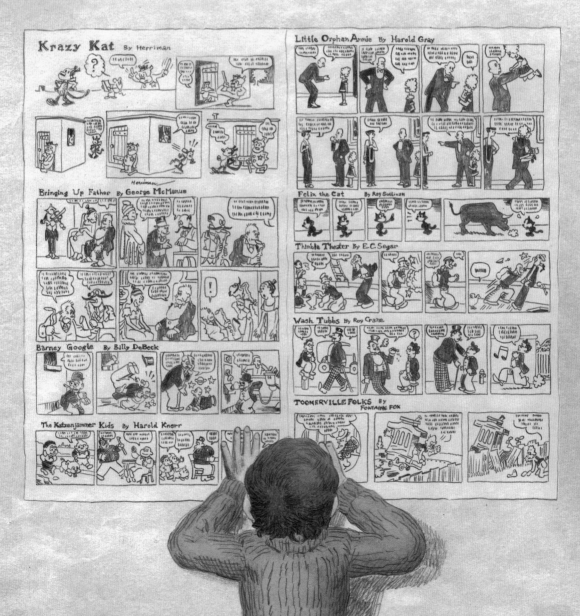

JAKOV, MEIN KIND, KOMM DA. GRUSS DEIN BEIBI BRUDER, DAVID.

HALLO, DAVID. ICH BIN JAKOV, DEIN GROSSER BRUDER.

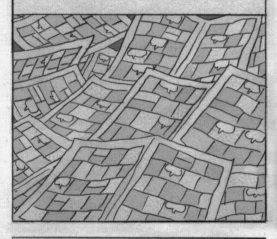

EVERYTHING IN MY NEIGHBORHOOD WAS GRAY AND DIRTY. THE ONLY COLOR CAME ON SUNDAYS.

MY VACATION WAS GOING UP ON THE FIRE ESCAPE AND SPREADING OUT THE SUNDAY COMICS SECTION.

I'D SPEND THE WHOLE DAY THERE. THE ADVENTURE STRIPS COMBINED WITH THAT EXTRA DIMENSION OF COLOR SET MY IMAGINATION ON FIRE.

TARZAN, PRINCE VALIANT, FLASH GORDON--THEY WERE MY ART EDUCATION. HAL FOSTER AND ALEX RAYMOND WERE MY TEACHERS.

JAKIE KURTZBERG!

HOW MANY TIMES DO I HAVE TO TELL YOU NOT TO SCRIBBLE ON THESE WALLS? YOU WANT I SHOULD THROW YOUR FAMILY OUT ON THE STREET?

LOOK AT ME WHEN I TALK TO YOU.

IS THERE A BLOCK FIGHT ON, JAKIE?

WE SHARED AN ALLEYWAY BORDER WITH THE ENEMY. GANG WAR COULD BREAK OUT AT ANY TIME. WE'D THROW BRICKS AND BOTTLES.

IT'S A BLOCK FIGHT! WE GOT A BLOCK FIGHT!

WE'D CHASE EACH OTHER UP AND DOWN FIRE ESCAPES, OVER THE ROOF, AND EVEN ACROSS CLOTHESLINES.

THE PUNCHES WERE REAL. THE ANGER WAS REAL. THE INJURIES WERE REAL, TOO.

THERE WAS AN UNSPOKEN STREET CODE. IF YOU KNOCKED SOMEBODY OUT, YOU DID YOUR BEST FOR THEM.

THEY KNOCKED ME OUT COLD AND CARRIED ME HOME. THEY STRAIGHTENED MY CLOTHES AND MADE SURE I LOOKED OKAY.

THEY DIDN'T WANT MY MOTHER TO BE TOO SHOCKED WHEN SHE FOUND ME.

MY MOTHER WAS A NATURAL STORYTELLER. SHE'D TELL US "VUNDER-MEYSES" OR "WONDER STORIES" FROM THE OLD COUNTRY.

WHEN THE KING DIED, HIS DAUGHTER SAID SHE WOULD MARRY THE STRONGEST, CLEVEREST MAN IN THE COUNTRY. A GREAT WRESTLING MATCH WAS HELD.

TWO TAILOR'S APPRENTICES CAME TO COMPETE. THEY WERE LAUGHED AT.

THE ELDER APPRENTICE DEFEATED THE CHAMPION WRESTLER.

THE YOUNGER APPRENTICE DEFEATED THE REST.

I LEARNED TO TELL MY MOTHER'S STORIES. THE RABBI HAD ME TELL THEM IN FRONT OF MY CLASS AT HEBREW SCHOOL.

TO DECIDE BETWEEN THEM, THE PRINCESS TOLD THE ELDER APPRENTICE TO BRING HER THE MOON.

SHE TOLD THE YOUNGER TO BRING HER A CHARCOAL FROM THE SUN.

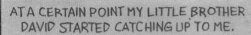

AT A CERTAIN POINT MY LITTLE BROTHER DAVID STARTED CATCHING UP TO ME.

I TOLD YOU, JAKIE!

I'M BIGGER THAN YOU.

SAY! WHAT GIVES?

BEFORE LONG, PEOPLE STARTED THINKING I WAS HIS BABY BROTHER.

MY MOTHER DRESSED HIM LIKE LITTLE LORD FAUNTLEROY. MOST OF THE FIGHTS I GOT INTO WERE A RESULT OF ME TRYING TO PROTECT HIM.

HE GOT ME OUT OF A COUPLE SCRAPES. HE SAW MY LEGS STICKING OUT OF A DOGPILE AND PULLED ME OUT.

ONE DAY COMING OUT OF P.S. 20...

THAT'S HOW I DISCOVERED THE PULPS--*WONDER STORIES* PUBLISHED BY HUGO GERNSBACK.

IT WAS MY GATEWAY TO ANOTHER WORLD. I BECAME A FANATICAL LIFELONG COLLECTOR.

I HAD TO KEEP IT A SECRET. PEOPLE THOUGHT YOU WERE THE VILLAGE IDIOT IF YOU READ THOSE THINGS.

BUZZZZZZZ

WHAT'S THAT NOISE?

DON'T WORRY. IT'S JUST AN AIRPLANE.

IT WAS THE FIRST TIME ANY OF US HAD EVER SEEN AN AIRPLANE.

THERE IT IS!

I CAN SEE IT!

EVERYBODY WANTED TO GET A LOOK. SOME GUY REALLY SHOVED ME OUT OF THE WAY.

GANGWAY! I WANNA SEE!

DON'T SHOVE ME!

I KNOCKED HIM CLEAN OUT.

MY PARENTS ENROLLED ME IN ART CLASSES AT PRATT INSTITUTE. I LASTED ONLY A WEEK.

MY FATHER LOST HIS JOB, SO WE COULDN'T AFFORD THE TUITION.

I HAD TO PITCH IN. I GOT A JOB AS A NEWSBOY. YOU HAD TO FIGHT YOUR WAY PAST A CROWD OF KIDS.

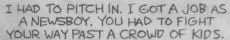

WATCH YOUR ELBOWS!

WAIT YOUR TURN LIKE EVERYBODY ELSE, SQUIRT.

GETCHA PAPER!

GIMME ONE, KID.

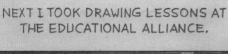

NEXT I TOOK DRAWING LESSONS AT THE EDUCATIONAL ALLIANCE.

YOU DRAW VERY FAST, JACOB.

TOO FAST. WHEN YOU'RE DRAWING WITH CHARCOAL, THE IMAGE SHOULD EMERGE SLOWLY.

YOU MIGHT BE BETTER SUITED TO A DIFFERENT MEDIUM.

בָּרוּךְ אַתָּה יְיָ אֱלֹהֵינוּ מֶלֶךְ הָעוֹלָם, אֲשֶׁר בָּחַר בָּנוּ מִכָּל הָעַמִּים, וְנָתַן לָנוּ אֶת תּוֹרָתוֹ. בָּרוּךְ אַתָּה יְיָ, נוֹתֵן הַתּוֹרָה.

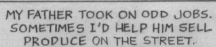

MY FATHER TOOK ON ODD JOBS. SOMETIMES I'D HELP HIM SELL PRODUCE ON THE STREET.

SAY, KID! HOW WOULD YOU LIKE TO BECOME A CITIZEN OF THE BBR?

THE BOYS BROTHERHOOD REPUBLIC WAS DIFFERENT FROM OTHER BOYS' CLUBS. IT WASN'T RUN BY GROWN-UPS. THE BOYS MADE THE RULES.

I'M LEON.

I'M MORRIS. PUT 'ER THERE.

IT WAS A MINIATURE CITY WITHIN THE CITY.

WE HAD OUR OWN ELECTED GOVERNMENT, OUR OWN COURTS OF LAW, OUR OWN MAYOR, OUR OWN CHIEF OF POLICE.

I MADE A COUPLE OF BUCKS AS AN ERRAND BOY FOR THE HEARST NEWSPAPERS.

MY BOSS AT THE PAPER SEEMED LIKE HE HAD AN EASY SETUP.

ME AND SOME PALS AT THE BBR STARTED A NEWSPAPER. I WAS THE EDITOR.

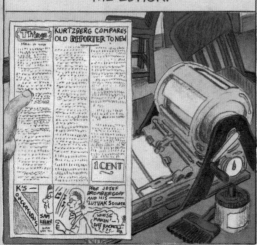

I WAS ALSO THE STAFF CARTOONIST.

IT WAS MY FIRST PUBLISHED WORK.

I WAS RAISED BY THE CINEMA. MY MOTHER USED TO COME THERE WHEN SHE WAS LOOKING FOR ME. I WATCHED CHAPLIN AND BUSTER KEATON.

I SAW THE MARX BROTHERS PERFORM LIVE AT THE ACADEMY OF MUSIC ON 14TH STREET, BEFORE THEY WERE FILM STARS.

DOUGLAS FAIRBANKS CORNERED THE SWASHBUCKLING HERO MARKET. ON ANY GIVEN WEEK HE COULD BE ZORRO, THE MAN IN THE IRON MASK, THE THIEF OF BAGDAD, OR ROBIN HOOD.

THE CRIME PICTURES, EVERY BIT AS FANTASTICAL, SEEMED CLOSER TO HOME. THESE WERE ATTAINABLE FANTASIES.

MY NEIGHBORHOOD PRODUCED REAL-LIFE GANGSTER TYPES AND THE ACTORS WHO PLAYED THEM.

I THOUGHT ABOUT GOING INTO THE RACKETS. I HAD A FRIEND WHO WENT THAT WAY AND GOT SHOT. I SAW WHAT IT DID TO HIS MOTHER.

I SERIOUSLY CONSIDERED GOING INTO SHOW BUSINESS. I NEEDED AN IRISH-SOUNDING NAME LIKE JIMMY CAGNEY. I TOLD MY MOTHER I WANTED TO GO TO HOLLYWOOD AND BE AN ACTOR.

NO.

VIOLENCE WAS WHAT WE KNEW, AND WE TOOK IT WITH US TO SCHOOL. ONE OF THE TEACHERS GOT US PLAYING BASKETBALL IN THE MORNING JUST TO WEAR US DOWN A LITTLE.

I USED TO HIDE BEHIND A BRICK WALL, WAIT FOR THREE GUYS TO PASS, AND I'D BEAT THE CRAP OUT OF THEM AND RUN LIKE HELL. AT THE BBR I CHANNELED MY MEANNESS IN THE GYM. I WAS A GOOD BOXER.

MY PAL MORRIS WAS AN AVIATION NUT. HE HAD HIS OWN PLANE HE MAINTAINED HIMSELF. HE TOOK ME UP IN IT ONCE. WE WERE HELD IN OUR SEATS WITH ROPES.

HE DID LOOPS OVER THE CITY. WE LAUGHED OUR ASSES OFF.

I TOOK A LOW LEVEL JOB AT MAX FLEISCHER STUDIOS, DOING CLEANUP FOR THE ANIMATORS. I WANTED TO DO MORE. I CAJOLED THEM INTO LETTING ME TAKE THE TEST TO BE AN IN-BETWEENER.

I HAD TO DRAW THE MOMENTS "IN BETWEEN" THE MAIN MOMENTS THE ANIMATORS DREW. I SPENT MY DAYS WORKING AT A LIGHT TABLE. THE WHOLE PLACE WAS ROWS AND ROWS OF GUYS WORKING AT LIGHT TABLES.

IT BEGAN TO LOOK A LITTLE TOO MUCH LIKE MY FATHER'S GARMENT FACTORY. I GOT BORED WITH IN-BETWEENING. I WANTED TO DRAW THE MAIN ACTION.

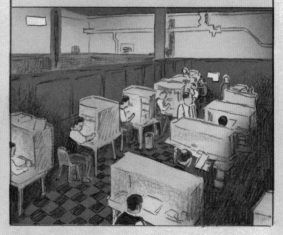

I WORKED MY WAY UP TO ASSISTANT ANIMATOR. ONE DAY, MAX FLEISCHER HIMSELF CAME INTO THE OFFICE. EVERYBODY MADE A BIG DEAL ABOUT IT.

:PSST: JAKE, IT'S HIM. IT'S MR. FLEISCHER.

THERE WAS TROUBLE FROM THE UNIONS, SO THEY MOVED THE STUDIO TO FLORIDA. I ASKED MY MOTHER IF I COULD MOVE TO FLORIDA WITH THEM. SHE SAID "NO," SO I HAD TO FIND OTHER WORK.

I GOT A JOB AT LINCOLN FEATURES, A TINY COMICS SYNDICATE RUN BY CARTOONIST HORACE T. ELMO.

WHERE ARE THE DRAWING TABLES? WHERE ARE ALL THE OTHER ARTISTS?

I DO MOST OF IT MYSELF AND FARM OUT THE REST TO GUYS LIKE YOU.

I GHOSTED HORACE "TEDDY" ELMO'S TWO-BIT POPEYE CLONE "SOCKO THE SEADOG." HE COPIED ELZIE SEGAR'S STYLE, AND I DID, TOO... AT FIRST.

BOP

BANG!!

THE FLIES AROUND THIS TUB SURE ARE A NUISANCE.

TEDDY

ALL OF ELMO'S STRIPS WERE COPIES OF WHATEVER WAS POPULAR.

I CONVINCED ELMO TO LET ME DO MY OWN ORIGINAL SCIENCE-FICTION ADVENTURE STRIP CALLED "CYCLONE BURKE."

"CYCLONE" BURKE   By Bob Brown

BOB BROWN

OUCH! YOU'LL REGRET THIS! YOU ANIMATED TEA KETTLE! — LET GO OF ME!!

CYCLONE'S SHOTS TAKE NO EFFECT UPON THE APPROACHING ROBOT WHO ADVANCES WITH LONG GLIDING STEPS AND —

GRIPS CYCLONE WITH HIS CRUSHING TENTACLE!

IT WAS A BUCK ROGERS/FLASH GORDON CONCEPT WITH A TIME TRAVEL ANGLE.

THE ASSIGNMENTS KEPT COMING AND I NEVER SAID "NO." I TOOK WHATEVER JOB I COULD GET, AND I DREW THEM ALL AT MY MOTHER'S KITCHEN TABLE.

CLEAR YOUR DRAWINKS, IT'S SUPPERTIME.

SURE THING, MA. I COULD USE A BREAK.

19

DO YOU KNOW WHAT PAPERS MY STRIPS ARE RUNNING IN? SO MY MOM CAN SEE THEM...

THEY'RE DOING WELL OVERSEAS, KID.

I WORKED ON A VARIETY OF STRIPS IN A VARIETY OF STYLES, UNDER A VARIETY OF PEN NAMES.

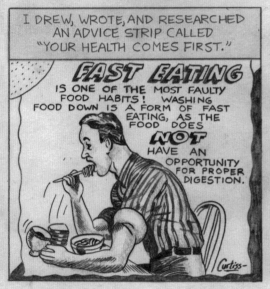

I DREW, WROTE, AND RESEARCHED AN ADVICE STRIP CALLED "YOUR HEALTH COMES FIRST."

FAST EATING IS ONE OF THE MOST FAULTY FOOD HABITS! WASHING FOOD DOWN IS A FORM OF FAST EATING, AS THE FOOD DOES NOT HAVE AN OPPORTUNITY FOR PROPER DIGESTION.

I DID POLITICAL CARTOONS.

WHAT THE HELL DO YOU KNOW ABOUT ANY OF THIS STUFF? YOU'RE JUST SOME PUNK KID TALKING ABOUT WORLD EVENTS.

KEEP UP THE GOOD WORK, KURTZBERG.

WITH THE EXTRA DOUGH I WAS PULLING IN, WE WERE ABLE TO MOVE INTO A HALF-DECENT PLACE IN BRIGHTON BEACH.

I'D BUILT UP A SOLID PORTFOLIO AND USED IT TO GET A JOB WORKING IN WILL EISNER AND JERRY IGER'S COMICS STUDIO.

EISNER AND IGER HAD A NO-NONSENSE ATMOSPHERE. THEY SAID "DO A STORY" AND YOU HAD TO DO THAT STORY. THEY GAVE YOU SUPERVISION.

THEY GAVE YOU GUIDELINES. WE LEARNED TO THINK FAST AND MEET DEADLINES. I WAS GETTING BETTER AND BETTER FROM THE COMPETITION.

THERE WAS A COMMUNITY OF ARTISTS. MORT MESKIN DID "SHEENA QUEEN OF THE JUNGLE." HE WAS SHY, BUT HIS ART WAS LIVELY.

BOB KANE DREW "PETER PUPP": A FUNNY ANIMAL STRIP WITH MACABRE VILLAINS AND GOTHIC DEATHTRAPS.

LOU FINE WAS LIGHT-YEARS AHEAD OF THE REST OF US, AND WE ALL WANTED TO LEARN HIS SECRETS.

GEORGE TUSKA WAS A MACHINE: QUIET AND EFFICIENT. HE DIDN'T TAKE ANYBODY'S SHIT.

LOU INKED MY FIRST "COUNT OF MONTE CRISTO" STRIP. I SAW WHAT HE DID TO MY PENCILS WITH SHADING AND ATMOSPHERE. I FOLDED THAT INTO MY STYLE ON "WILTON OF THE WEST" AND "DIARY OF DR. HAYWARD."

HA-HA-THAT WAS AS IT SHOULD BE. FOR A LAD OF ONLY 19 YOU ARE REMARKABLY ABLE TO HANDLE THE POSITION OF CAPTAIN, AND I THINK THAT YOU WILL REPLACE YOUR DEAD CAPTAIN

AY THIS UN DANTE'S PL AS ONE W AFFRONT

AFTER YEARS OF WORKING IN COMICS, I FINALLY SAW SOME OF MY WORK ON THE NEWSSTAND, ALL IN COLOR FOR A DIME.

JUMBO COMICS
Bigger and Better Funnies 10¢
HAWKS OF THE SEA
PETER PUPP
SHEENA
BIG PAGES - BIG PICTURES - BIG TYPE - EASY TO READ

COMICS

ALSO... PUZZLE PHUN, JOKES, MODERN PLANES, INSPECTOR DAYTON, COUNT OF MONTE CRISTO, WILTON OF THE WEST AND MANY OTHER FAVORITES
PRIZES — STORIES — FUN

SUPERMAN SAVED MY LIFE. IT WAS A SCI-FI STORY LIKE FLASH GORDON OR JOHN CARTER, BUT HE FOUGHT REAL PROBLEMS IN THE REAL WORLD, THE CROOKS AND THE POLITICIANS.

WE DO THE TOWEL SERVICE HERE. WHY ARE YOU UNHAPPY?

WE CAN USE ANY TOWEL SERVICE WE WANT.

SKRITCH SCRATCH

THAT'S WHERE YOU'RE WRONG. WE OWN THE TOWEL SERVICE. NOBODY ELSE SERVICES THIS BUILDING. YOU TAKE MY MEANING?

YOU GET THE HELL OUT OF HERE! WE DON'T WANT TO DEAL WITH YOU. THIS IS AMERICA.

KURTZBERG, GET BACK TO WORK.

LOOK, BUB! WE CAN TAKE ANYBODY'S TOWELS WE WANT. TAKE YOUR DIRTY SHMATAS AND SCRAM!

WHO IS THIS GUY? LOOK, I AIN'T LOOKIN' FOR NO TROUBLE. LET'S BE NICE.

KURTZBERG, LET ME TAKE CARE OF THIS.

SORRY, BOSS. YOU CAN'T LET THESE THUGS BULLY YOU. YOU CAN'T GIVE AN INCH.

1939 WORLD'S FAIR

THE NEW YORK WORLD'S FAIR PROVIDED ME WITH YEARS OF INSPIRATION.

THIS WAS THE BIRTHPLACE OF MY ASGARD AND MY NEW GENESIS.

THE THINGS I SAW AT THE WORLD'S FAIR STAYED WITH ME FOR THE REST OF MY CAREER.

THE FUTURAMA SHOWED ME A WORLD I WANTED TO INHABIT.

MEET... ELEKTRO!

SUPERMAN WAS A RUNAWAY HIT. EVERY PUBLISHER WANTED A SUPERMAN. EISNER AND IGER PUT OUT WONDER MAN FOR VICTOR FOX.

I DID BLUE BEETLE, WHICH HAD MORE IN COMMON WITH THE PRE-SUPERMAN HERO, THE PHANTOM. FOX HAD BIG PLANS, INCLUDING A RADIO SHOW.

IT'S KILLER CONWAY, ALRIGHT. —WONDER WHAT HE'S UP TO?

THE STUDIO GOT CAUGHT IN THE MIDDLE OF A LAWSUIT BETWEEN FOX AND SUPERMAN'S PUBLISHER.

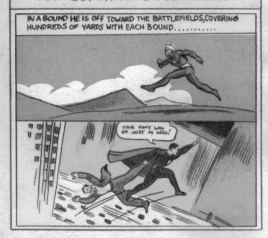

IN A BOUND HE IS OFF TOWARD THE BATTLEFIELDS, COVERING HUNDREDS OF YARDS WITH EACH BOUND............

YOUR FOOT WILL DO JUST AS WELL!

FOX LOST THE LAWSUIT. EISNER AND IGER LOST THE FOX ACCOUNT.

LOOK, KURTZBERG, WE CAN'T AFFORD YOU ANYMORE. FOX IS SORE AT US OVER WONDER MAN. MAYBE YOU CAN GO WORK DIRECTLY FOR HIM?

I STARTED WORKING IN FOX'S STUDIO, AN EVEN BIGGER OUTFIT THAN EISNER AND IGER.

I MET AL HARVEY THERE. THIS WAS BEFORE HE STARTED HIS OWN COMICS EMPIRE.

VICTOR FOX WAS A CHARACTER.

I'M THE KING OF COMICS!

WE'D IMITATE HIS CATCHPHRASE AND LARGER-THAN-LIFE MANNERISMS BEHIND HIS BACK.

I WAS STILL MOONLIGHTING, TAKING WHATEVER JOB I COULD FROM OTHER STUDIOS AFTER EIGHT HOURS AT THE OFFICE.

I WAS BURNING THE MIDNIGHT OIL, LOTS OF LATE NIGHTS.

I DID A STRIP CALLED "SOLAR LEGION." I'M A SCIENCE FICTION NUT. I DO MY BEST ON EVERY JOB, BUT MY SCI-FI STRIPS ALWAYS HAD A LITTLE SOMETHING EXTRA.

UNFOUNDED, WHIC... THE VAST FRONTIER... YET UNBORN.....

By JACK KIRBY

THIS WAS THE FIRST TIME I SIGNED A STORY AS "JACK KIRBY," BUT THE PUBLISHER REMOVED THE SIGNATURE BEFORE IT SAW PRINT.

ALMOST ELUDED ME, DIDN'T YOU, ELRAMIS, MY DEAR. SURPRISED, MR. CARSON? OH YES, YOUR LOVELY, LITTLE FRIEND IS INDEED THE NOTORIOUS SPACE PIRATE

JACOB, I WANT YOU TO MEET OUR NEW EDITOR.

JACOB KURTZBERG, MEET JOE SIMON.

JOE WAS ALWAYS IN MOTION, ALWAYS GETTING THINGS DONE. HE SEEMED LIKE A GROWN-UP EVEN THOUGH HE WASN'T MUCH OLDER THAN ME.

HOW'S THE EXTRA WORK COMING, AL?

IT'S A LOT, JOE. I'M GONNA NEED MORE TIME. MAYBE A DAY OR TWO?

HEY, JOE. I HEARD YOU TALKING TO AL ABOUT EXTRA WORK. YOU GOT SOMETHING GOING ON THE SIDE?

YOU'RE NOT GONNA SAY ANYTHING TO FOX, ARE YOU?

HELL NO! I MOONLIGHT ALL THE TIME MYSELF. I JUST WONDERED IF YOU HAD ANYTHING EXTRA FOR ME?

LET'S GET LUNCH, JAKE.

FOUR DESSERTS? AREN'T YOU GOING TO GET ANY REAL FOOD?

CHOCOLATE CAKE IS REAL FOOD.

BREAK

CAFE

OPEN

YOU'RE GOOD, JAKE. YOU'RE FAST. YOU'VE GOT A REAL FLAIR FOR COMICS. I'VE GOT SOMETHING PERFECT FOR YOU. THE "SATURDAY EVENING POST" PEOPLE WANT TO GET INTO THE FUNNYBOOK BUSINESS.

JOE'S "BLUE BOLT" WAS RIGHT UP MY ALLEY--A FLASH GORDON TYPE WITH SUPERPOWERS IN A SCIENTIFICALLY ADVANCED UNDERGROUND KINGDOM.

I WOULD'VE TAKEN ANYTHING, BUT I WAS HAPPY TO WORK ON THIS ONE.

I CAME UP WITH A BOATLOAD OF IDEAS TO PUNCH IT UP AND HIT THE GROUND RUNNING.

YOU'LL HAVE TO DO BETTER THAN THAT, YOU BLOOD-THIRSTY DEMONS!

THE BLUE BOLT THROWS HIS ATTACKER INTO THE FACES OF THE OTHERS.

THERE'S A FAMILY MOVINK IN NEXT DOOR. THEY'VE GOT TWO DAUGHTERS.

LOOK, MA. THE WHOLE NEIGHBORHOOD'S TESTING OUT THE FURNITURE.

ME AND JOE STARTED WORK ON A NEW SUPERHERO THAT COMBINED ELEMENTS OF BATMAN AND SUPERMAN.

THE LESS SAID ABOUT THIS ONE, THE BETTER.

I DID A COMIC CALLED "MERCURY." IT WAS A SETUP I'D USE AGAIN AND AGAIN--ANCIENT GOD RETURNS TO EARTH TO FIGHT A MODERN THREAT, PULLED FROM THE HEADLINES.

MERCURY FINDS A COUNCIL OF THE GODS AWAITING HIM AS MAJESTIC JUPITER OUTLINES THE TASK THE FLEET YOUNG GOD MUST FULFILL

LONG HAVE I HOPED FOR THIS CHANCE. I GO!

SO ONCE AGAIN AN LEAVES OLYMPUS FOR WORLD OF MAN~ TO SAVE A CIVILIZATION GONE MAD...

THE DARK GOD PLUTO TOOK THE FORM OF HITLER, BUT WE GAVE HIM A PHONY NAME. AMERICA HADN'T ENTERED THE WAR YET.

S SEARCH FOR HIS EVIL COUSIN TO PRUSSLAND WHOSE PEOPLE R THE DICTATORIAL RULE OF EADER, RUDOLPH HENDLER !!

MERCURY INSTANTLY RECOGNIZES HIS INFAMOUS RELATIVE !!! MORTAL EYES CAN ONLY SEE HENDLER, THE FIERY, FUMING DICTATOR WHEREAS MERCURY'S CELESTIAL GAZE CAN EASILY PIERCE PLUTO'S MORTAL CLOAK

PRUSSLAND OVER THE WORLD

"COMET PIERCE" WAS ANOTHER ONE OF MY SIGNATURE SPACE JOCKEY JOBS. I SIGNED IT "JACK KIRBY."

IF YOU'VE REGAINED THE USE OF YOUR FACULTIES, MISTER PIERCE, LISTEN SHARPLY FOR MY MEN AND I HAVE NO TIME TO WASTE

THE NAME FINALLY MADE IT TO PRINT.

LIKE WITH "BLUE BOLT," I CAME IN ON ONE OF JOE'S CREATIONS CALLED "THE FIERY MASK." I FILLED IT WITH NIGHTMARES: SERIAL-KILLER DEMONS...

SUDDENLY THERE IS MOVEMENT~

THE TINY FACE PEERS ABOUT THE DARKENED ROOM! ITS EYES BLAZE WITH AN EERIE GLOW~ THE ANGELIC EXPRESSION IS GONE~IN ITS PLACE IS AN EVIL, MALIGNANT LEER.

...AND MURDEROUS BABIES WHO CLIMB OUT OF THEIR CRIBS AND KILL YOU IN YOUR SLEEP. WE DID IT FOR TIMELY, WHO PUBLISHED SOME OF THE MORE LURID PULP MAGAZINES.

ANTAGONISTS ARE AND THE STRANGE REGION HE'S IN

THE FIERY MASK FOLLOWS THE DEMONS BACK TO HELL AND KICKS THEIR ASSES.

WHEN JOE AND I PUT TOGETHER "MARVEL BOY" WE USED A LOT OF THE SAME ELEMENTS. THIS TIME IT WAS HERCULES VERSUS MARS, THE GOD OF WAR.

— AND HIS POWER-MAD VOICE ECHOES THROUGHOUT THE WORLD!

WAR WAR WAR WAR WAR WAR

...WHILE IN AMERICA A NEW LIST OF WORDS ARE ADDED TO THE VOCABULARY OF THE PEACE-LOVING PEOPLES OF THE NEW WORLD...WORDS SUCH AS—

INSTEAD OF COMING UP WITH A PHONY NAME, WE REFERRED TO HITLER AS THE "UNNAMED DICTATOR" IN THE SCRIPT.

FIFTH COLUMN-- THE TREACHEROUS ESPIONAGE SYSTEM AT WORK AGAINST A NEUTRAL NATION----

FIRST FRANCE, THEN BRITAIN-AND ULTIMATELY COMPLETE DOMINATION OF THE WORLD IS OUR AIM. AMERICA? THAT WILL BE EASY. THAT WILL BE AN INSIDE JOB!

UP IN VALHAL DECIDE

TRUE, BRAVE HERCULES! BUT IF YOU ARE RE-BORN IT WILL BE MANY YEARS BEFORE YOUR NEW FORM WOULD REACH MANHOOD- MANY DANGEROUS YEARS!

ALL THE MORE REASON TO ACT AT ONCE!

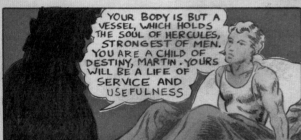

YOUR BODY IS BUT A VESSEL, WHICH HOLDS THE SOUL OF HERCULES, STRONGEST OF MEN. YOU ARE A CHILD OF DESTINY, MARTIN. YOURS WILL BE A LIFE OF SERVICE AND USEFULNESS

ON YOUR STRONG SHOULDERS RESTS THE FATE OF YOUR RACE

YOU ARE A MERE BOY, MARTIN, APPARENTLY INNOCENT AND HARMLESS. YOU SHALL CAUSE THE DOWNFALL AND DESTRUCTION OF MEN WHO HOLD POWER OVER MILLIONS. WHO DESPITE EVERY RESOURCE AT THEIR COMMAND SHALL MEET DEFEAT BY YOUR HANDS...YOU SHALL BE THE MARVEL OF YOUR AGE- THE BOY WITH THE STRENGTH OF TWENTY MEN -- THE MARVEL BOY

ALL RIGHT, PULL OVER, YOU DOGS!

MARTIN GOODMAN LIKED WHAT JOE WAS DELIVERING SO MUCH THAT, WHEN HE STARTED DOING COMICS IN-HOUSE AT TIMELY, HE MADE JOE THE EDITOR.

JOE AND I RENTED A ROOM WHERE WE DID OUR SIDE WORK AFTER OUR DAY JOBS, MINE AT FOX, HIS AT TIMELY.

YOU SHOULD QUIT FOX AND WORK WITH ME.

I GOT A GOOD THING WITH FOX. WHO KNOWS HOW LONG MARTIN'S COMICS WILL LAST?

BESIDES, I'M UP TO MY EYEBALLS IN WORK FOR LINCOLN FEATURES.

YOU'RE STILL DOING THAT PENNY-ANTE ELMO SHIT?

LOOK, JAKE, I CAN GET YOU ENOUGH MONEY THAT YOU CAN STOP DOING THE NICKEL-AND-DIME STUFF AND STILL COME OUT AHEAD.

JOE BROUGHT ME OVER TO TIMELY AS ART DIRECTOR, HIS RIGHT-HAND MAN. HE RAN THE COMICS PRODUCTION HOUSE INSIDE MARTIN GOODMAN'S MAGAZINE OPERATION.

MEET JAKE, MY ART DIRECTOR.

ARTIE GOODMAN WAS JOE'S PAL. THEY'D GO HORSE-BACK RIDING.

UNCLE ROBBIE KEPT TELLING US HOW TO MAKE COMICS, BUT HE DIDN'T KNOW SHIT.

ABE GOODMAN WAS MARTIN'S OLDEST BROTHER. HE DID BOOKKEEPING.

DAVE GOODMAN PHOTOGRAPHED GIRLS AND SAID HE'D MAKE THEM INTO MOVIE STARS.

SUB-MARINER AND HUMAN TORCH WERE TIMELY'S BIG STARS, BUT THEY WERE BEING PRODUCED BY AN OUTSIDE SUBCONTRACTOR, FUNNIES, INC.

MARVEL

22 PAGES OF *SIZZLING BLAZING ACTION!*

"NAMOR THE SUB-MARINER" WAS A HALF-MERMAN ANTIHERO FROM ATLANTIS CREATED BY BILL EVERETT FOR A MOVIE THAT NEVER HAPPENED. WILLIAM BLAKE EVERETT WAS A DESCENDANT OF POET WILLIAM BLAKE.

HE BASED THE COMIC ON "RIME OF THE ANCIENT MARINER" BY SAMUEL COLERIDGE. BILL WAS VERY ERUDITE.

CARL BURGOS WAS RESPONSIBLE FOR TIMELY'S OTHER HIT, "THE HUMAN TORCH." MARTIN WAS TRYING TO WRANGLE THE COPYRIGHTS AWAY FROM FUNNIES, INC.

OUR JOB WAS TO MAKE A HIT COMIC IN-HOUSE SO HE WOULDN'T HAVE TO RELY ON AN OUTSIDE COMPANY.

I GOT ALL THE WORK I COULD HANDLE: COMIC BOOK COVERS, LIKE THIS ONE FOR "THE ANGEL," AND ILLUSTRATIONS FOR MARTIN'S PULPS.

WE WERE BUSTING OUR HEADS TO COME UP WITH AN ORIGINAL CONCEPT, SOMETHING DIFFERENT FROM THE RUN-OF-THE-MILL SUPERHEROES.

WHAT IF HIS POWERS COME FROM SMOKE?

ANYWHERE THERE'S SMOKE, HE CAN ESCAPE INTO IT AND ENTER THE FOURTH DIMENSION.

SMOKE IS OUR LINK TO THE SUPERNATURAL, IT'S WHERE OUR WORLD AND THE OTHER WORLD MEET. HE IS A CREATURE OF THAT DIMENSION. ANYWHERE THERE'S SMOKE, HE CAN DISAPPEAR INTO IT.

"AND ANYWHERE THERE'S SMOKE HE CAN JUMP OUT OF IT AND GRAB YOU... AND PULL YOU INTO HIS WORLD. HE'S NOT QUITE AN ANGEL AND NOT QUITE A DEVIL."

THE VISION

I THINK WE GOT SOMETHING HERE.

THIS MUST BE THE TENTH GUY WE'VE DONE WITH WINGS ON HIS HEAD.

DO YOU THINK HE NEEDS A CAPE?

I'M THINKING WE CALL HIM "SUPER-AMERICAN!"

HOW ABOUT "SUPER-LAWSUIT?"

SOMETIMES YOU KNOW WHEN YOU HAVE A HIT. THIS WAS MY FIRST TIME.

THE DEADLINE'S COMING UP, JACK. LET ME PUT AL AVISON AND AL GABRIELE ON A COUPLE OF THE STORIES.

HELL NO, JOE! I'M DOING THIS ONE MYSELF.

IT WAS THE RIGHT BOOK FOR THE RIGHT TIME. THIS IS WHAT WAS ON PEOPLE'S MINDS.

RECRUITMENT STATION

FUEHRER'S PLANS!

AMERICAN MUNITIONS INC.

THE RESULTING WAVE OF SABOTAGE AND TREASON PARALYZES THE VITAL DEFENSE INDUSTRIES!

EVERY OTHER SUPER CHARACTER WAS JUST A COMIC BOOK. THIS WAS REAL LIFE. THE PRESIDENT SAID SO RIGHT ON PAGE TWO.

S -- IT'S ...ELESS!

WHAT WOULD YOU SUGGEST, GENTLEMEN? A CHARACTER OUT OF THE COMIC BOOKS? PERHAPS THE HUMAN TORCH IN THE ARMY WOULD SOLVE OUR PROBLEM!

THE DOOR SLOWLY OPENS, AND A GNARLED, BONY HAND REACHES FOR A WAITING AUTOMATIC...THEN RECOGNIZING THE VISITORS -- REPLACES THE FIRE-ARM!

THE FORMULA HAS BEEN FOUND..., THEY ARE WAITING FOR YOU NOW!

I PUT EVERYTHING I HAD INTO THAT COMIC: POLITICS, ESPIONAGE, SCIENCE FICTION, ADVENTURE AND MYTHOLOGY.

THE ARMY OFFICIALS GASP IN STARTLED AMAZEMENT AS THE WRINKLED OLD SHOP-KEEPER SHEDS HER WIZENED FEATURES TO BECOME AN ASTOUNDINGLY BEAUTIFUL YOUNG WOMAN.

GROVER AND HIS PRETTY AGENT SILENTLY MOTION THE

CAPTAIN AMERICA WAS MY STORY. A SICKLY KID WHO FOUGHT TWICE AS HARD AS THE BULLIES OF THE WORLD.

A SIDE DOOR OPENS...AND A FRAIL YOUNG MAN STEPS INTO THE LABORATORY...

DON'T BE AFRAID, SON... YOU ARE ABOUT TO BECOME ONE OF AMERICA'S SAVIORS!

CAP WAS MEANT TO BE THE FIRST OF A NEW BREED OF SUPERMAN, BUT ENDED UP BEING ONE OF A KIND.

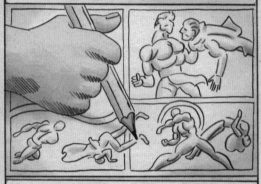

I DREW WHAT I KNEW. I COMPOSED VIOLENT BALLETS.

WE KNEW WE HAD SOMETHING. JOE NEGOTIATED A PIECE OF THE ACTION FOR US ON EVERY COPY SOLD.

CAPTAIN AMERICA CAPTURES SPY

CAPTAIN AMERICA NABS SPY!

EXPLOSION

CAPTAIN AMERICA... NATION'S NO. 1

CAPTAIN AMERICA NEEDED A PARTNER, OTHERWISE HE'D JUST BE TALKING TO HIMSELF THE WHOLE TIME. EVERY KID COULD IMAGINE HIMSELF AS BUCKY.

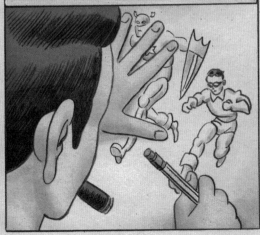

THIS WAS THE FIRST TIME WE CALLED HITLER OUT BY NAME--NOT A STAND-IN.

THE COVER OF "CAPTAIN AMERICA COMICS" #1 FEATURED THE FUTURISTIC NEW INVENTION OF TELEVISION.

CAPTAIN AMERICA HAD A GIRLFRIEND, AGENT X-13, BETTY ROSS—ONE LETTER AWAY FROM "BETSY ROSS."

WELL WELL...IF I HAVEN'T STUMBLED INTO A SKUNK'S NEST!

HELPLESSLY GRIPPED BY TWO BURLY NAZIS!

BETTY ROSS IS THE NAME, CAPTAIN..IT SEEMS WE BOTH HAVE AN INTEREST IN THE SAME CASE.

AIN'T SHE PRETTY, CAP?

L PAY THAT HERR AIN ICA LOW RE!

SO YOU'RE ONE OF THE PHEWRER'S FLUNKIES, EH SANDO?

THE NAME IS VON KRANTZ...AND I PLAN A CHAIN OF DISASTERS THAT WILL DESTROY THE MORALE OF YOUR WHOLE COUNTRY!

A HERO IS NOTHING WITHOUT A VILLAIN, AMERICA.

IN A SECLUDED SECTION OF TOWN, A WEIRD FIGURE APPROACHES A CHESSBOARD...
SO ADMIRAL PERKINS

THE RED SKULL WAS THERE FROM THE VERY FIRST ISSUE. HE WAS THE NAZI EQUIVALENT OF CAPTAIN AMERICA, A VILLAIN DEDICATED TO VILLAINY.

I DIDN'T KNOW IT THEN, BUT I'D BE TELLING THE STORY OF THE DEATH DANCE BETWEEN THESE TWO AT EVERY STAGE OF MY CAREER.

ON THE CONTRARY—WE'LL HOLD HIM AS HOSTAGE...THEN HE SHALL LOOK THROUGH MY EYE AT DEATH!

KNOCK! KNOCK!

IT'S ME, YOU SAP!

I DID TWO BACKUPS IN ISSUE ONE. HURRICANE WAS THE SON OF THOR, GOD OF THUNDER, FIGHTING HIS ANCESTRAL ENEMY, PLUTO—THE DEVIL.

THE VANDERPONT MANSION RESOUNDS TO DEAFENING, BLOOD-CHILLING BATTLE CRIES. HURRICANE AND THE DEVIL RUSH EACH OTHER IN A FURIOUS HEAD ON CHARGE!!!

THE OTHER BACKUP, TUK CAVEBOY, IS ABOUT A YOUNG GOD RAISED BY CAVEMEN. "TUK" MEANS "AVENGER," THAT MAKES HIM THE FIRST AVENGER.

FROM THE DARK AGES

AK, THE LAST OF THE SHAGGY ONES, CALLED HIM TUK, BUT THE BOY DIDN'T REALIZE THAT "TUK" MEANT "AVENGER" AND THAT HE WAS DESTINED TO ROAM THE PREHISTORIC WILDS OF 50,000 B.C. IN SEARCH OF "ATTILAN," ISLAND OF THE GODS TO RECLAIM A LOST THRONE...

I KNOW YOU, CUB, THAT OLD AK'S BODY

JOHN GOLDWATER, WHO RAN ARCHIE, THREATENED A LAWSUIT BECAUSE HE FELT CAPTAIN AMERICA WAS TOO SIMILAR TO HIS SHIELD CHARACTER.

INTRODUCING **THE SHIELD!** G-MAN EXTRAORDINARY

10¢ 64 PAGES ALL COLOR

Also— BENTLEY OF SCOTLAND YARD

MARTIN TOOK US DOWN TO THE ARCHIE OFFICES TO TRY TO IRON OUT THE SITUATION.

AFTER THE MEETING, GOLDWATER PULLED JOE ASIDE AND TRIED TO HIRE US AWAY FROM GOODMAN.

THE END RESULT WAS THAT I HAD TO START DRAWING CAP'S SHIELD ROUND SO IT DIDN'T LOOK SO MUCH LIKE THE SHIELD'S INSIGNIA.

DIDN'T THINK THAT LOVE TAP WOULD STOP ME, DID YOU?

POW!

-TAT

THIS IS MARTIN'S NEPHEW, STANLEY. HE'S THE NEW OFFICE BOY.

GOOD TO MEET YA.

HOW DO YOU DO, KID?

SEEMS LIKE EVERYBODY HERE IS A RELATIVE BUT ME AND JOE.

THE ONLY REASON I CALL HIM "UNCLE MARTIN" IS BECAUSE HE'S MARRIED TO MY COUSIN. WE'RE NOT REALLY NOTHIN'.

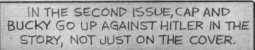

IN THE SECOND ISSUE, CAP AND BUCKY GO UP AGAINST HITLER IN THE STORY, NOT JUST ON THE COVER.

WHAT IS THIS? HEY! WHAT 'CHA DOING?

HOLD STILL BUCKY FIRST I'M GOING TO DRESS YOU UP!

...THEN I DRESS MYSELF UP. OUCH! EASY WITH THAT CORSET!

...AND NOW WE'RE GOING TO EUROPE!

AW SHUCKS!

THEY COULDN'T TRAVEL FREELY THROUGH EUROPE, SO THEY HAD TO ADOPT NEW SECRET IDENTITIES.

YOU GET THE BIG ONE ADOLPH, I'LL GET THE LITTLE GUY

NO, HERMANN I'LL GET THE LITTLE GUY!

THIS TIME WE DECIDED CAP SHOULDN'T DIRTY HIS GLOVES SLUGGING HITLER AND GOERING.

ARE YOU BOTH SATISFIED?

WHOOSH!

WE THOUGHT IT WOULD BE BETTER TO TREAT THEM LIKE CLOWNS AND HAVE CAP'S BOY TAKE THEM DOWN.

WE KNEW THE BOOK WAS A SMASH WHEN THE APPLICATIONS FOR MEMBERSHIP IN THE "SENTINELS OF LIBERTY" STARTED POURING IN.

CAPTAIN AMERICA'S SENTINELS OF LIBERTY

1. IN GOD WE TRUST
2. ALLEGIANCE TO THE FLAG AND THE CONSTITUTION OF THE UNITED STATES OF AMERICA
3. TO MAKE MYSELF A BETTER CITIZEN AND DEFEND MY GOVERNMENT FOREVER.

CAPTAIN AMERICA

SENTINELS OF LIBERTY

WE HAD A ROOM WHERE ME AND JOE WOULD MEET WITH WRITERS.

RED SKULL PICKS UP A BOMB AND HURLS IT--

SAY, FELLAS! CAN I HELP? WHY DON'T YOU LET ME WRITE A STORY?

STANLEY, AMSCRAY!

STANLEY WAS A BOTHER. HE'D HOP AROUND THE OFFICE PLAYING HIS FLUTE.

HE LIKED TO IRK PEOPLE, OPENING AND CLOSING DOORS ON YOU.

HEE HEE

SLAM

SORRY!

LOOK, STANLEY, WHY DON'T YOU WRITE THE FILLER STORY THIS ISSUE? WE NEED A TWO-PAGE PULPER.

GEE, BOSS, THAT STUFF'S FOR MUGS, BUT YOU KNOW WHAT, I'LL DO IT AND I'LL KNOCK YOUR SOCKS OFF.

STANLEY WROTE A TEXT PIECE THAT RAN IN THE THIRD ISSUE, USING HIS PEN NAME, STAN LEE. WE CALLED THEM NOVELETTES.

CAPTAIN AMERICA FOILS the TRAITOR'S REVENGE By Stan Lee

I DID THE ILLUSTRATIONS THAT ACCOMPANIED THE STORY. I GUESS YOU COULD CALL IT ME AND STANLEY'S FIRST COLLABORATION.

BEFORE I MET JACK, I WAS WORKING AS A LINGERIE DESIGNER, DOING FINE WORK, DRAWING THE LACE PATTERNS.

MEET ROSALIND GOLDSTEIN

MY FAMILY MOVED INTO THE APARTMENT ABOVE JACK'S FAMILY.

LOTS OF GIRLS WERE INTERESTED IN JACK. EVERYBODY WAS STARTING TO CALL HIM "KIRBY" AROUND THAT TIME.

WHEN I MOVED IN, THE NEIGHBORS HAD FIVE DAUGHTERS, AND EVERY ONE OF THEM WAS AFTER JACK.

WHEN I FIRST MET JACK, MY PARENTS AND HIS PARENTS WERE GETTING ACQUAINTED. HE WAS PLAYING STICKBALL WITH HIS FRIENDS.

GOOD GAME, FELLAS.

WOULD YOU LIKE TO SEE MY ETCHINGS?

OH... SURE.

WHAT COULD HAPPEN? MY FOLKS WERE THERE. HIS FOLKS WERE THERE.

I WAS DISAPPOINTED. I THOUGHT HE WANTED TO FOOL AROUND. IT WAS THE FIRST TIME I SAW CAPTAIN AMERICA. I'D NEVER READ A COMIC BOOK IN MY LIFE.

HE SAYS HE WANTS TO. TALK TO THE ARTIST FROM CAPTAIN AMERICA.

I'LL TAKE THAT, ELSIE.

YEAH, I'M THE GUY WHO DRAWS CAPTAIN AMERICA. OH YEAH? YOU'RE GONNA KICK MY ASS? I'LL BE WAITING FOR YOU DOWNSTAIRS, SMART GUY!

I WAITED OUT FRONT, BUT HE DIDN'T SHOW UP.

THE THREATENING TELEPHONE CALLS CONTINUED. SHADY CHARACTERS STARTED COMING OUT OF THE WOODWORK

HITLER DID NOT ATTACK US WHY ATTACK HIM?

WHY NOT DEFEND AMERICA FIRST LEAVE GERMANY ALONE

TRUE AMERICANISM

SIGN-CARRYING PROTESTERS FROM THE GERMAN AMERICAN BUND STARTED PICKETING THE BUILDING.

HELLO? SPEAKING. OH! YES, OF COURSE. I'M FOND OF YOUR WORK AS WELL.

PSSST! IT'S THE MAYOR.

MAYOR LAGUARDIA WAS A COMICS FAN. HE USED TO READ THE FUNNIES ON THE RADIO FOR THE KIDS.

WNYC

HE TOLD US TO KEEP DOING WHAT WE'RE DOING. FROM THEN ON WE HAD POLICE PROTECTION.

SIMON AND KIRBY WERE IN DEMAND. WE RENTED AN APARTMENT WHERE WE WORKED NIGHTS ON THE SIDE JOBS JOE WOULD LINE UP FOR US.

JACK, YOU THINK YOU COULD COPY THIS STYLE?

CHILD'S PLAY.

GOSH, JOE, THESE SCRIPTS STINK. CAN'T WE PUNCH 'EM UP LIKE WE USUALLY DO?

SORRY, JACK, THE CLIENT WAS VERY SPECIFIC. FAWCETT HAS A FORMULA AND THEY WANT US TO STICK TO IT.

BESIDES, THERE'S NO TIME.

IT'S BAD ENOUGH THEY'RE MAKING US STICK WITH THIS ROTTEN DRAWING STYLE. WHY WOULD THEY WANT US TO DRAW BAD ON PURPOSE?

ANY LAST WORDS TO SAY?

MY LAST WORDS WON'T BE SAID FOR A LONG TIME YET!

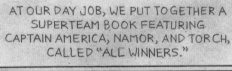

IF WE CAN'T CHANGE IT, HOW 'BOUT WE DON'T SIGN OUR NAMES TO IT.

MY THOUGHTS EXACTLY.

AT OUR DAY JOB, WE PUT TOGETHER A SUPERTEAM BOOK FEATURING CAPTAIN AMERICA, NAMOR, AND TORCH, CALLED "ALL WINNERS."

SUDDENLY FROM NOWHERE AN ARMY OF ZOMBIES EMERGES FROM HIDING...

KILL!

KILL!

KILL!

KILL KILL

IN THE FIRST ISSUE THEY FOUGHT AN ARMY OF UNDEAD ZOMBIES.

WE DID ANOTHER TEAM BOOK CALLED "THE YOUNG ALLIES," FEATURING ALL THE SIDEKICKS: BUCKY, TORO, AND A KID GANG LIKE THE ONE I USED TO BE IN.

THE ACCOUNTANT AT MARVEL PULLED US ASIDE.

LOOK, BOYS. I DON'T KNOW WHAT MARTIN'S BEEN TELLING YOU, BUT HE OWES YOU A TON OF MONEY FROM CAPTAIN AMERICA.

BUT HE SAID IT'S BARELY BREAKING EVEN.

CAPTAIN AMERICA IS A BONA FIDE HIT. HE'S MAKING MILLIONS ON IT. HE PROMISED YOU A PERCENTAGE. HE OWES YOU A FORTUNE.

HE'S PUTTING ALL THE EXPENSES OF THE COMPANY ON CAPTAIN AMERICA JUST BECAUSE IT'S THE ONE BOOK WHERE HE OWES A ROYALTY. IT'S AN OLD TRICK.

I CAN'T BE A PARTY TO IT.

WE TALKED TO JACK LIEBOWITZ AT DC/NATIONAL. HE WELCOMED US WITH OPEN ARMS.

WELCOME TO THE FAMILY, GENTLEMEN.

SIMON AND KIRBY AT NATIONAL!

HAVE A STOGIE.

ONE THING, MR. LIEBOWITZ. I KNOW YOU PUBLISHERS ALL SOCIALIZE WITH EACH OTHER. GOODMAN DOESN'T KNOW WE'RE HERE. LET'S KEEP IT THAT WAY.

FIVE HUNDRED SMACKERS A MONTH! ALL THAT **AND** A PERCENTAGE!

WE'LL SEE IF WE GET ANY OF IT.

ONE TIME JACK TOOK ME HORSEBACK RIDING IN CENTRAL PARK. IT WAS JOE SIMON'S IDEA.

JOE INTRODUCED JACK TO CIGARS, FINE SUITS, AND NOW HORSES.

JACK COULDN'T GET HIS HORSE TO MOVE. I COULDN'T STOP LAUGHING.

IF YOU THINK THIS IS BAD, YOU SHOULD SEE ME ON A BICYCLE.

JACK NEVER LEARNED HOW TO RIDE A BIKE. I WAS GOING TO TEACH HIM.

HE JUST COULDN'T FOCUS ON THE SIMPLE TASK AT HAND. HIS HEAD WAS CONSTANTLY IN ANOTHER WORLD.

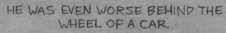

HE HIT A TRUCK AND ENDED UP IN THE BACK OF A HORSE-DRAWN CART. DON'T ASK ME HOW HE MANAGED THAT.

HE WAS EVEN WORSE BEHIND THE WHEEL OF A CAR.

CIRCULATION STARTED HITTING 900,000. JOHN GOLDWATER FROM ARCHIE WAS SORE BECAUSE WE WERE OUTSELLING HIS SHIELD CHARACTER.

WE HAD A NEW CAPTAIN AMERICA VILLAIN CALLED "THE HANGMAN."

HE THREATENED TO SUE OVER SIMILARITIES TO HIS SUPERHERO, HANGMAN.

THE CHARACTERS WERE NOTHING ALIKE, BUT HE SEEMED EVEN MORE INTENT ON TAKING LEGAL ACTION.

WE FOUND OUT GOODMAN AND GOLDWATER HAD A HISTORY. THEY BOTH WORKED FOR HUGO GERNSBACK.

JOHN. MARTIN

WE'VE GOTTA STOP MEETING LIKE THIS.

STOP RIPPING OFF MY CHARACTERS.

YOU'RE JUST JEALOUS.

GERNSBACK PUBLISHED THE SCI-FI PULPS OF MY YOUTH. THINGS GOT TENSE. MARTIN AGREED TO NEVER USE THE HANGMAN AGAIN. THAT WAS FINE WITH ME AND JOE. DONE DEAL.

STAN BROUGHT HIS KID BROTHER LARRY TO THE TIMELY OFFICE. THE KID WAS A CAPTAIN AMERICA FAN AND AN ASPIRING ARTIST IN HIS OWN RIGHT. HE REMINDED ME OF MY LITTLE BROTHER DAVID.

WOW-EE! YOU GUYS INVENTED CAPTAIN AMERICA?

I DREW A SKETCH FOR HIM. IT WAS THE FIRST OF MANY PIECES OF ART I DREW FOR FANS.

GEE! STANLEY, LOOKEE!

TO LARRY

— JACK KIRBY

IN "CAPTAIN AMERICA" #5, WE WENT DIRECTLY FOR THE GERMAN AMERICAN BUND. WE LET THEM KNOW WE WEREN'T AFRAID OF THEIR THREATS.

I AM OF GERMAN DESCENT. YES! — BUT I'M ALSO A GOOD AMERICAN CITIZEN! I'LL HAVE NOTHING TO DO WITH AN ORGANIZATION THAT AIMS TO DESTROY THE COUNTRY THAT PROTECTS ME AND MINE FROM CREEPS LIKE YOURS!!

WH-WHAT ARE YOU GOING TO DO?

UGH-H!

HIT HIM HARDER! HE'S NOT UNCONSCIOUS YET.

I DON'T WANT YOU GOING WITH NOBODY ELSE NO MORE.

THAT DUD THAT ME AND JOE DIDN'T PUT OUR NAMES ON BECAUSE WE THOUGHT IT WOULD LAY AN EGG...

64 Pages of New CAPTAIN MARVEL Adventures

...IT WAS ONE OF THE BEST-SELLING COMICS OF THE DECADE.

CAPTAIN AMERICA WAS STILL GOING STRONG, BUT AFTER THE "HANGMAN" BROUHAHA, WE DECIDED NOT TO CALL OUR NEW VILLAIN "THE BAT."

THE BLOW-GUN CERTAINLY DONE DE'TRICK, EH TOAD?

IT WAS AN EXCELLENT JOB! I'LL SEE THAT THE BADGERS NEVER WIN AGAIN!

UNKNOWN TO THE TOAD AND HIS MEN, THEIR HIDEOUT HAS BEEN DISCOVERED--

SOON THE BADGERS WILL BE ON THE MARKET AS A JINX TEAM! THEY'LL BE SHUNNED AND BROKEN

MEET YOUR JINX, TOAD!

OW!

I WAS MAKING COMICS FASTER THAN I COULD THINK, AND I WAS HAVING A BALL.

WE PUT TOGETHER AN ORIGINAL CONCEPT FOR NATIONAL PERIODICAL PUBLICATIONS, CALLED "SUPER SHERLOCK," BUT NOTHING EVER CAME OF IT.

They asked if we could sprinkle some of our S + K magic on their failing "MANHUNTER" strip.

We obliged. We rebuilt it from the ground up into a state-of-the-art "long underwear" book.

National loved what we did with Manhunter--

Say, fellas! Whatcha talking about?

UH...

Nothing, Stanley. Give us a minute.

Shit, Joe! You think the kid heard us?

So what if he did, Jack?

National asked us to do the same thing with Sandman, who was looking a little long in the tooth, like an old pulp hero.

We gave him a new costume and a kid sidekick like Bucky, in one issue they fought Thor.

WE WERE INNOVATING. NATIONAL WAS GIVING US BETTER PAY THAN GOODMAN.

I'VE HEARD OF HIM BUT I DON'T BELIEVE ANY SUCH PERSON EXISTS.

IT'LL BE A TOUGH CLIMB ARE YOU GAME SANDY?

I'M GAME FOR ANYTHING, SANDMAN.!!

...G IN THE BARREL OF THE PISTOL. THE WIREPOON IMBEDS ITSELF IN ...HE OPPOSITE BUILDING... AS THE WIRE CABLE SNAPS TAUT!

THIS BUTTON REELS IN WIRE

REEL OF FINE BUT TOUGH WIRE

TRIGGER RELEASES WIRE

STEEL BARB FITS BARREL BORE WHEN NOT RELEASED

HOW THE WIREPOON GUN WORKS!

RING GRIP USED BY SANDMAN WHEN REELED IN... WIRE PULLS HIM TOWARD OBJECTIVE!

IS EVERYTHING GOOD, GENTLEMEN? ARE YOU HAPPY WITH HOW YOU'RE TREATED HERE?

SURE, ROBBIE. IT'S GREAT HERE.

WHY DO YOU ASK?

YOU THINK MARTIN GOODMAN IS A SUCKER? HE KNOWS ALL ABOUT YOUR OTHER JOB.

ROBBIE, WHAT'RE YOU GOING ON ABOUT?

YOU LIKE WORKING FOR THE COMPETITION? THERE'S THE DOOR. YOU'RE FIRED!

FIRED? YOU'RE REALLY SERIOUS.

WHERE DO YOU THINK YOU'RE GOING? YOU'VE STILL GOT THAT ISSUE OF CAPTAIN AMERICA TO FINISH! AND DON'T SKIMP ON THE DETAIL JUST 'CUZ YOU'RE CANNED.

SO WE SAT DOWN AND GOT BACK TO WORK ON OUR LAST JOB FOR MARTIN, "CAPTAIN AMERICA" #10. WE WERE PROS.

I NOTICED STANLEY IS NOWHERE TO BE FOUND TODAY. YOU THINK HE RATTED US OUT TO THE BOSS?

WHO THE HELL KNOWS, JACK?

WELL I KNOW IF I EVER SEE THAT GUY AGAIN I'LL FUCKIN' KILL HIM.

AS NARRATED TO "JOE SIMON" AND "JACK KIRBY"

MISTER KIRBY.

MISTER SIMON,

WE WENT OVER TO NATIONAL PERIODICAL PUBLICATIONS FULL-TIME, AND CAME UP WITH THE "NEWSBOY LEGION," BASED ON ME AND MY PALS.

THERE WERE KID GANGS IN THE PICTURES, BUT I HAD FIRSTHAND EXPERIENCE. WE DIDN'T HAVE A SUPERHERO IN OUR CREW, THOUGH.

WE STRUCK GOLD WITH ANOTHER KID GANG, THE BOY COMMANDOS. THEY RAISED HELL IN EUROPE INSTEAD OF IN THE NEIGHBORHOOD,

ROBIN AND I WANT TO WELCOME YOU BOY COMMANDOS TO DETECTIVE COMICS!

GEE! THANKS BATMAN. WE'RE GLAD TO BE IN SUCH GOOD COMPANY!

YOU FELLOWS ARE A SWELL BUNCH OF HARD-HITTING CHARACTERS AND—WHEN YOU HAVE TERRIFIC ADVENTURES!

THE TIMELY SUBJECT MATTER MADE THE BOY COMMANDOS A RUNAWAY HIT. AT ONE POINT IT WAS NATIONAL'S THIRD BEST-SELLING BOOK.

THEY'RE BACK!! THE YEAR'S MOST SENSATIONAL NEW HEROES IN FOUR COMPLETE STORIES STRAIGHT OUT OF THE HEADLINES

LET'S GIVE ADOLF THE BUM'S RUSH WITH WAR BONDS AND STAMPS!

AT NATIONAL I MET THE EDITOR, MORT WEISINGER. WE HAD A LOT IN COMMON. WE SHOULD'VE BEEN FRIENDS, BUT HE WAS NEVER GONNA LET THAT HAPPEN.

SO THIS IS THE "GREAT" SIMON AND KIRBY?

I CAN'T SAY I'M IMPRESSED.

HE WAS THE SON OF AUSTRIAN-JEWISH PARENTS. HIS FATHER WAS IN THE SHMATA BUSINESS, LIKE MINE, BUT HIS WAS MORE IN THE MANAGEMENT END OF THINGS.

HE WAS A BRONX KID WHO DREAMED OF SOMETHING MORE.

LIKE ME, HE WAS A FAN OF THE SCIENCE FICTION MAGAZINES. HE WAS DIRECTLY INVOLVED IN THE BEGINNING OF ORGANIZED SCI-FI FANDOM AND CO-CREATED "TIME TRAVELLER," THE FIRST SCI-FI FANZINE.

IT WAS IN THE SCI-FI FANDOM THAT YOUNG MORT MET YOUNG JULIUS SCHWARTZ. THEY STARTED A LITERARY AGENCY SPECIALIZING IN SCI-FI AND FANTASY, THE FIRST OF ITS KIND. "CAPTAIN MARVEL" WRITER OTTO BINDER WAS ONE OF THEIR FIRST CLIENTS. THEY EVENTUALLY REPPED H. P. LOVECRAFT AND RAY BRADBURY.

WEIRD TALES

20¢

A THRILLER
THE SHADOW OVER INNSMOUTH
by H. P. LOVECRAFT

WEISINGER LEFT THE AGENCY AND BECAME EDITOR OF SUPERMAN AND BATMAN AT NATIONAL. HE WAS NONE TOO PLEASED HAVING OUR "BOY COMMANDOS" UPSTAGE BATMAN IN DETECTIVE COMICS, EVEN MORE SO WHEN "BOY COMMANDOS" GOT ITS OWN BOOK AND STARTED OUTSELLING HIS.

HE CO-CREATED A SLEW OF NEW CHARACTERS, INCLUDING AQUAMAN AND GREEN ARROW. HE WAS TERRITORIAL AND PRICKLY. WE NEVER WORKED UNDER HIM, BUT THE GUYS THAT DID SAID HE WAS PRONE TO ABUSIVE VERBAL OUTBURSTS AND MANIPULATIVE MIND GAMES.

DECEMBER 7, 1941. JAPAN BOMBED THE U.S. NAVAL BASE AT PEARL HARBOR.

THE NEXT DAY, WE WERE AT WAR.

...A DAY WHICH WILL LIVE IN INFAMY.

COMICS IS A YOUNG MAN'S BUSINESS, AND YOUNG MEN WERE GETTING DRAFTED.

WE GOT TO WORK BUILDING UP A BACKLOG OF MATERIAL. I PUT TOGETHER MODEL SHEETS OF OUR CHARACTERS SO THE OTHER ARTISTS COULD TAKE OVER IF ME AND JOE LEFT.

BROOKLYN

TEX

OUR STUDIO WAS IN A RACE AGAINST THE DRAFT BOARD IN ADDITION TO THE NORMAL RACE AGAINST DEADLINES. LIFE WENT ON.

I TOOK ROZ ROLLER-SKATING.

NO TALE OF WOE HERE. I WAS DYNAMITE ON A PAIR OF SKATES.

THE DAY BEFORE OUR WEDDING, JACK WAS RUNNING SOME ERRANDS. HE HAD THE DOG WITH HIM AND IT THREW UP.

SHIT!

SCREEEE

KSHHH!!

WALKING DOWN THE STREET ON OUR WAY TO THE RECEPTION STRANGERS STARTED YELLING AT JACK.

SLACKER!

BOO!

WHY ARE YOU STILL HERE? WHY AREN'T YOU IN THE WAR LIKE THE REST OF THE BOYS?

WE HAD A HUNDRED PEOPLE AT THE RECEPTION AND RECEIVED LOTS OF CASH, BUT WE DIDN'T WANT TO SPEND ANY OF IT ON OUR HONEYMOON BECAUSE WE NEEDED TO FURNISH THE HOUSE. WE TOLD EVERYONE WE WERE GOING DOWN SOUTH FOR THE HONEYMOON, BUT JUST STAYED HERE.

THE NEXT DAY I RAN INTO A NEIGHBOR AT THE LOCAL MARKET.

I THOUGHT YOU WERE ON YOUR HONEYMOON.

OH, WE FORGOT A FEW THINGS AND HAD TO COME BACK.

AFTER THAT WE DIDN'T SHOW OUR FACES FOR THE REST OF THE WEEK.

JACK WASN'T DRAFTED BECAUSE HE WAS SUPPORTING TWO HOUSEHOLDS.

GERMAN SUBMARINES WERE SINKING SHIPS OFF THE ATLANTIC COAST. GERMAN SUBS WERE EVEN IN THE HUDSON RIVER.

JACK WAS AN AIR RAID WARDEN. WE'D STAY UP UNTIL 3:00 AM IN OUR CIVIL DEFENSE UNIFORMS.

GET YOUR WINDOW SHADES DOWN!

JACK ALWAYS FOUGHT WITH MY LITTLE SISTER. HE DIDN'T LIKE THE GUYS SHE WENT OUT WITH.

WHAT DO YOU WANT?

I'M HERE FOR ANNIE. YOU HER BRUDDA?

"BROTHER-IN-LAW" AND YOU'RE SITTING IN MY CHAIR.

WHAT DA!?

GET THE HELL OUT OF HERE AND DON'T COME BACK!

YOU GOT A SCREW LOOSE, BUB!

WHAT'S ALL THE RACKET?

WHY DID YOU DO THAT? HE WAS MY DATE!

HE'S A BUM! YOU DON'T WANT NOTHING TO DO WITH HIM.

ROZ! WHY DID YOU MARRY THIS HEEL!? HE'S RUINING MY LIFE!

MY SISTER WAS FURIOUS WITH JACK, I THOUGHT SHE WAS GOING TO KILL HIM.

I WAS ONE OF THE FEW YOUNG MEN LEFT. A YOUNG MAN NOT IN UNIFORM WAS A CONSPICUOUS SIGHT.

SLACKER!

ALL THE BOYS ARE OFF FIGHTING HITLER! WHAT'S YOUR EXCUSE!? YOU SHOULD BE ASHAMED OF YOURSELF!

YOU COWARD!

EVERYBODY HAD BEEN CALLING ME "KIRBY" FOR A WHILE SO I DECIDED TO LEGALLY CHANGE MY NAME.

Kurtzberg
Former Name

Kirby, Jack
New Name

IT'S ONLY A MATTER OF TIME, SO I'M DOING IT ON MY OWN TERMS.

I GUESS THIS IS THE END OF SIMON AND KIRBY?

BEST OF LUCK!

JOE GOT A GOOD POSITION IN THE COAST GUARD BECAUSE OF HIS HORSEMANSHIP. IT TURNS OUT HE WAS ABLE TO KEEP MAKING COMICS, TOO.

THE ARMY SENDS YOU TWO LETTERS. ONE TO TELL YOU YOU'RE DRAFTED. ONE TO TELL YOUR FAMILY YOU'RE DEAD. I GOT THE FIRST ONE, DAYS BEFORE MY NAME CHANGE WENT INTO EFFECT.

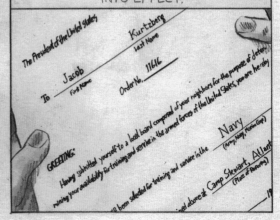

MY CARD WAS STAMPED "NAVY." SOME GUY CAME IN AND SAID "WE NEED SIX GUYS FOR THE ARMY." I FEEL I WAS MEANT FOR THE NAVY, BUT BEING A LOSER, I WAS PICKED FOR THE ARMY.

I WAS DRAFTED, BUT I DIDN'T MIND GOING. IT WAS THE THING TO DO. ALL MY FRIENDS WERE GONE, EVEN JOE. MORT WEISINGER WAS ON THE BUS. THAT WAS A BAD OMEN. HE WAS THERE JUST TO TICK ME OFF, I'M SURE.

ROZ MOVED BACK IN WITH HER PARENTS, AND I WAS AT CAMP STEWART, OUTSIDE ATLANTA.

I WAS ASSIGNED TO ARTILLERY. WE DID TARGET PRACTICE. MY GROUP WAS A MOTLEY CREW. WE WERE LIKE THE KEYSTONE COPS.

WE MISSED THE TARGET, BUT SHOT DOWN THE PLANE THAT WAS TOWING IT. THE PILOTS HAD TO BAIL OUT.

I GOT REASSIGNED TO THE MOTOR POOL AS A MECHANIC. I DIDN'T KNOW WHAT I WAS DOING. WHEN SOMEBODY CAME BY, I'D JUST START BANGING THE UNDERSIDE OF THE JEEP AND PRETEND I WAS FIXING SOMETHING.

LOOK, THIS IS ALL A BIG MISTAKE. I SHOULDN'T EVEN BE HERE. I DRAW CAPTAIN AMERICA. I SHOULD BE DOING WORK FOR MILITARY PUBLICATIONS.

IS THAT SO?

I GOT A MENTION IN THE CAMP STEWART NEWSPAPER. THAT WAS IT. THEY REASSIGNED ME TO RIFLEMAN.

I HATED IT THERE, AND THEY ALWAYS GAVE ME A HARD TIME.

YOU'D GET TEN YEARS FOR PUNCHING A SERGEANT, SO I COULDN'T PUNCH A SERGEANT.

THEY'D WAKE US UP AT TWO IN THE MORNING AND MAKE US HIKE 50 MILES, WITH A FULL PACK, A RIFLE, AND EVERYTHING ELSE ON ROADS ROUGH AS HELL.

I TOOK JUDO. I WAS GOOD. OUT OF A CLASS OF 27, JUST ME AND ANOTHER FELLOW GRADUATED.

I MET SOUTHERNERS FOR THE FIRST TIME. I DIDN'T KNOW ANYBODY WHO SPOKE LIKE THAT. I BEGAN TO GET A FEEL FOR THE UNITED STATES IN A WAY I NEVER HAD BEFORE.

ROZ AND HER 16-YEAR-OLD SISTER MADE THE TRIP DOWN SOUTH TO VISIT. ROZ WANTED ME TO SET HER SISTER UP ON A DATE.

I INTRODUCED HER TO A GUY IN MY BARRACKS WHO WAS FROM TEXAS. THEY TOOK A LIKING TO EACH OTHER AND WENT OUT ON A DATE.

HE GAVE ME AN EARFUL.

THAT SISTER-IN-LAW OF YOURS TOLD A NEGRO WOMAN TO SIT RIGHT DOWN NEXT TO HER. THE DRIVER THREW THE BOTH OF THEM RIGHT OFF THE BUS. I PRETENDED I DIDN'T KNOW HER. ARE ALL NEW YORK GIRLS THAT CRAZY? WE JUST DON'T DO THAT DOWN HERE.

I TRIED FIXING HER UP WITH MY SERGEANT, MORRIS. HE WAS ABOUT TEN YEARS OLDER THAN HER.

THEY WERE OIL AND WATER. THEY WENT OUT ON A DATE AND THEY FOUGHT THE WHOLE TIME. THEY BOTH SWORE NEVER TO SEE EACH OTHER EVER AGAIN. I WASN'T GOING TO DO ANY MORE MATCHMAKING.

SO HOW'D IT GO?

I DON'T WANT TO TALK ABOUT IT, KURTZBERG.

IN AUGUST THEY SHIPPED US OUT. WE WERE SENT TO THE POINT OF EMBARKATION. WE WERE STUFFED INTO THIS BIG CROWDED SHIP. THE SHIP SWAYED BACK AND FORTH ACROSS THE ATLANTIC. WE WERE ESCORTED BY "BABY BATTLESHIPS" AND LARGE CRUISERS.

WE REACHED ENGLAND AT NIGHTFALL, LANDING IN LIVERPOOL. THE CITY WAS IN RUINS, STILL SUFFERING FROM THE BLITZ. THE PEOPLE WERE SLEEPING IN THE SUBWAYS.

WE WEREN'T THERE LONG BEFORE THEY MOVED US OUT OF LIVERPOOL TOWARD GLOUCESTER. I REMEMBER A LOT OF MARCHING AND WAITING.

WE WERE TRAMPING THROUGH THE STREETS ON OUR WAY TO SOUTHAMPTON, WHICH IS THE PORT OF EMBARKATION TO NORMANDY.

I GOT A GLIMPSE OF THE ENGLISH COUNTRYSIDE WHEN WE REACHED THE EMBARKATION AREA NEAR DARTMOUTH. IT WAS LIKE A GARDEN. IT WAS THE MOST BEAUTIFUL THING I'D EVER SEEN.

WE WERE THERE FOR A FEW DAYS AND GOT ON A BOAT FOR FRANCE.

OMAHA BEACH, 1944

IT WAS TEN DAYS AFTER D-DAY. THEY HADN'T FINISHED CLEANING THE PLACE UP. I ARRIVED ON AN LST LANDING CRAFT. WHEN I GOT THERE, BODIES WERE LYING IN HEAPS.

THERE WERE BODIES FROM THE INVASION THAT WERE STILL THERE. WE MOVED QUICKLY INTO THE HEDGEROW COUNTRY AND INTO WAITING TRUCKS.

THE VILLAGES WE DROVE THROUGH WERE IN RUINS. YOU COULD SEE THE FORMER BEAUTY OF THESE PLACES.

I NEVER GOT TO SEE PARIS. WE BYPASSED THE CITY. WE JOINED THE FORCES THAT WERE BEING GATHERED FOR GENERAL PATTON.

I CAN'T REMEMBER WHAT HAPPENED YESTERDAY, BUT I CAN RECALL THE FACES OF EVERYBODY THAT WAS IN MY UNIT. OUT OF 1,000 MEN, ONLY ME AND FOUR OTHER GUYS CAME OUT.

MOST AMERICANS HAVE AN IMAGE OF WAR, ESPECIALLY THAT WAR, THAT IT WAS A CAREFULLY PLANNED EVENT, PROFESSIONAL SOLDIERS MOVING IN COLUMNS, AIMING THEIR RIFLES.

WE WERE HOLDING A BRICK FACTORY AND SPENT THE NIGHT THERE. I SLEPT IN THE OVEN BECAUSE IT WAS WARM, THE BRICKS WERE HOT. I COULD'VE COME OUT A COOKIE.

I WAS TALKING TO A GUY IN MY UNIT. HE MADE LIEUTENANT IN THE ROTC IN COLLEGE. HE WAS FROM BROOKLYN, SO WE HAD SOMETHING IN COMMON. WE WERE TALKING ABOUT HOME.

NEXT THING I KNOW, I'M ALL THE WAY UP ON THE FOURTH FLOOR. NO SOUND, NOTHING, JUST KNOCKED INTO THE FACTORY.

THE GUY I WAS TALKING TO IS A SMEAR ON THE WALL ACROSS THE STREET. YOU DON'T GET MORE UNDIGNIFIED THAN THAT.

I SEE THE THREE TANKS COMING UP THE STREET WITH INFANTRY ON EACH SIDE. HE TOOK A DIRECT HIT.

I WAS A VETERAN FIVE MINUTES AFTER I GOT THERE. THE S.S. BUSTED THROUGH THE DOOR LIKE AN ERROL FLYNN PICTURE. THERE'S A GUY RUNNING AT YOU WITH A SCHMEISSER AND IT'S POINTED AT YOUR HEAD AND THIS GUY LOOKS LIKE A BUTCHER.

FIRE, KIRBY!

I SAID "FIRE!"

HE'S GOT ALL THE ACCOUTREMENTS ON HIM AND HE'S GONNA KILL YOU. I DIDN'T KNOW WHAT TO DO UNTIL A SERGEANT HIT ME ON THE BACK OF THE HELMET WITH HIS.

FIRE!!!

IT'S A MACK TRUCK AND YOU CAN'T GET OUT OF THE WAY. HE'S GOT HIS GUN ON YOU, YOU'VE GOT YOUR GUN ON HIM. WHAT DO YOU DO? SO I SHOT A GUY.

WE WERE ALL FIRING OUT THE WINDOWS. WE HAD TWO WOUNDED GUYS, ALL BANDAGED UP, WAITING FOR A JEEP TO TAKE THEM.

NEXT THING WE KNOW, THE WOUNDED GUYS ARE DEAD AND WE HAVE A BUNCH MORE INJURED.

THE GERMANS CAME CHARGING IN. ONE OF THEM WAS RUNNING AT ME.

SOME GUY FROM THE SECOND FLOOR SHOT HIM. HE WENT FLYING THROUGH FOUR ROOMS. THE PICTURES ARE SPILLING OUT OF HIS HAT.

PICTURES OF HIM IN THE HITLER JUGEND. PICTURES OF HIS MOTHER. PICTURES OF HIS GIRLFRIEND. HIS WHOLE LIFE. IT WAS ALL IN HIS HELMET.

I WALKED INTO THIS TOWN WHERE THEY HAD A COMMAND CENTER. MY REPUTATION PRECEDED ME.

PRIVATE KIRBY?

YESSIR.

JACK KIRBY THE ARTIST?

YES, SIR! I DRAW CAPTAIN AMERICA.

AND BOY COMMANDOS?

YES, SIR!

SO YOU CAN DRAW?

YES, SIR!

I'M MAKING YOU A SCOUT. HERE'S A MAP. I WANT YOU TO GO INTO THESE TOWNS WE DON'T HAVE AND SEE IF ANYBODY IS THERE. DRAW MAPS AND PICTURES OF WHAT YOU SEE.

COME BACK AND TELL US IF YOU FIND ANYTHING.

:GULP:

SO I WAS A SCOUT. IF SOMEBODY WANTS TO KILL YOU, THEY MAKE YOU A SCOUT. I'D WALK INTO THESE TOWNS AND IT WAS LIKE SOMETHING OUT OF A MOVIE. BURNT-OUT BUILDINGS, SHATTERED RUBBLE EVERYWHERE.

I WENT INTO THIS ONE VILLAGE TO SCOUT FOR GERMANS. IT WAS A BOMBED-OUT RUIN. I LOOKED IN THE WINDOWS AND THERE WAS NOTHING.

I CAME TO THIS FRENCH HOTEL. IT HAD A BIG WINDING STAIRCASE IN THE LOBBY--PROBABLY A SWANKY PLACE WHERE ALL THE SWELLS WENT TO PICK UP GIRLS.

SORTEZ LES MAINS EN L'AIR!

KOMM MIT DEN HÄNDEN HOCH!

COME OUT WITH YOUR HANDS UP!

COME OUT WHERE I CAN SEE YOU!

THIS BIG DOG CAME OUT FROM BEHIND A PILE OF RUBBLE. IT WAS CUT AND BURNED ALL OVER.

IT STOPPED IN FRONT OF ME AND JUST STARED. IT JUST LOOKED AT ME WITH THESE DEEP ACCUSING EYES. IT WAS THE MOST HUMAN EXPRESSION I'VE EVER SEEN ON AN ANIMAL.

THE DOG STARED AT ME ACCUSINGLY, LIKE HE WAS SAYING, "YOU! YOU DID THIS TO ME." I FELT SO GUILTY.

HE WAS SKINNY AND SCRAWNY BUT HE HAD HUMAN EYES. I THOUGHT HE WAS GOING TO START SPEAKING.

WE WERE CAMPED OUT BY A BIG RAVINE. YOU COULDN'T HEAR A THING. THE WIND WAS ROARING LOUD BOOMING SOUNDS.

THE C.O. CAME OUT OF THE TENT YELLING. THROUGH ALL THE NOISE WE COULDN'T HEAR A THING HE WAS SAYING.

HE JUST KEPT SCREAMING. EVENTUALLY HE JUST GAVE UP AND THREW HIS HANDS IN THE AIR.

WE MARCHED DOWN THE HILL.

I REALIZED THE SOUNDS WE WERE HEARING WEREN'T THE WIND. IT WAS TANKS AND SHELLS EXPLODING.

IT WAS A MASSACRE. WE WERE CAUGHT IN A TANK BATTLE. GUYS HAD THEIR CLOTHES BLOWN OFF. THEY WERE RUNNING NAKED ACROSS THE RIVER.

A GERMAN GUY RAN UP TO ME AND TRIED TO SURRENDER. HE HAD HIS SHIRT BLOWN OFF.

NICHT SCHIESSEN! ICH ERGEBE MICH.

I TOLD HIM TO GET THE HELL OUTTA HERE.

IT WAS JUST INSANITY.

THERE WAS A RING OF GERMAN SOLDIERS. JUST THE TOPS OF THEIR BODIES, LYING IN A RING, LIKE A FLOWER.

WHEN YOU'RE AN ARTIST YOU SEE THESE THINGS. PATTERNS IN THE CHAOS.

I SAW PATTON ONCE. HE WAS SCREAMING AT A GUY-- REALLY FOAMING AT THE MOUTH.

MOTHER FUCKER! WHY AREN'T THESE MEN DEAD?

THESE MEN ARE SUPPOSED TO BE DEAD. SOMETHING WENT TERRIBLY WRONG IF THESE MEN ARE STILL ALIVE.

YOU FUCKED UP MY PLAN!

HE WAS TALKING ABOUT US. WE SHOULD'VE BEEN DEAD. I THOUGHT, "WELL, FUCK YOU, I'M ALIVE."

I GOT A LETTER FROM ROZ. A FLOWERY BEAUTIFULLY WRITTEN LETTER. I READ IT OUT LOUD TO THE BOYS.

I AM THE NIGHT AND YOU THE DREAM. YOU ARE THE MOON AND I AM THE STREAM.

THEY ALL LAUGHED. I DID, TOO.

HAW HAW HAW

AFTER EVERYTHING WE'D BEEN THROUGH, IT SEEMED LIKE IT WAS FROM ANOTHER PLANET.

WHILE I WAS GETTING SHOT AT BY REAL NAZIS, CAPTAIN AMERICA WAS GETTING SHOT AT IN THE MOVIES. IT WAS A LOW-BUDGET STINKER.

ME AND JOE DIDN'T GET A DIME FROM IT, AND OUR NAMES WERE NOWHERE ON IT.

DURING A FIREFIGHT A GUY CRAWLED UP TO ME. HE GRABBED MY FEET. I ALMOST SHOT HIM. HE SAID, "PICK OUT FIVE MEN AND GO SEE MARLENE DIETRICH." THIS WAS WHILE THE FIGHTING WAS GOING ON.

YOU'RE OUT OF YOUR MIND. REPORT TO THE DOCTOR.

IF YOU DON'T WANT THIS DETAIL, I'LL GET ANOTHER GUY.

WE CRAWLED 100 YARDS, THEN WALKED 400 YARDS TO A TRUCK. WE LOADED ON WITH A BUNCH OF OTHER GUYS. THEY TOOK US SEVEN MILES DOWN THE ROAD AWAY FROM THE ACTION.

I SAW BING CROSBY AND MARTHA RAYE. MARLENE DIETRICH CAME OUT IN G.I. UNDERWEAR. BOMBS WERE GOING OFF ALL AROUND US, BUT AFTER A WHILE WE FORGOT ABOUT THE WAR.

A MAN'S BRAINS SPLATTERED ALL OVER THAT DRAWING. ANOTHER KIND OF GUY MIGHT'VE SAVED THAT DRAWING OUT OF MORBID INTEREST, BUT I'M NOT THAT KIND OF GUY.

I TORE THAT PAGE OUT OF THE BOOK AND THREW IT AWAY.

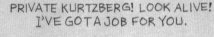

PRIVATE KURTZBERG! LOOK ALIVE! I'VE GOT A JOB FOR YOU.

MY COMMANDING OFFICER TOLD ME TO GET A PRISONER INTO A TRUCK. HE WAS AN OFFICER, AN S.S. MAN.

GET IN THE TRUCK.

LOOK AT YOU. YOU LOOK LIKE A PRICK.

YOU'RE COVERED WITH MUD. YOU LOOK LIKE GARBAGE. YOUR UNIFORM LOOKS LIKE SHIT! YOU'RE A DISGRACE TO YOUR ARMY. LOOK AT ME. MY UNIFORM IS PRESSED. THREE MEN WORKED ON MY BOOTS THIS MORNING.

HAVE YOU NOTHING TO SAY FOR YOURSELF?

CLICK CLICK

≥GRUMBLE≤ ≥GRUMBLE≤

THE GERMANS WERE PRETTY BOYS, Y'KNOW WHAT I MEAN? MORE THAN ONCE I HEARD THEM SAY, "WE MAKE BETTER SOLDIERS THAN YOU GUYS."

ONE TIME ON PATROL I SAW A GERMAN SOLDIER RIDING BY ON A BIKE.

BANG

ONE OF OUR GUYS SHOT HIM. DON'T ASK ME WHY, BUT ALL HELL BROKE LOOSE. SUDDENLY WE WERE GETTING SHOT AT BY A BUNCH OF HIS FRIENDS WHO JUST CAME OUT OF NOWHERE.

THIS IS HOW THINGS HAPPENED BACK THEN. THEY'D YELL AT YOU. BEFORE YOU KNOW IT, THEY'RE SHOOTING AT YOU.

AND THEN YOU'RE IN A FIREFIGHT.

ONE TIME I WAS ON PATROL, CHECKING OUT A TOWN. I WENT IN A HOTEL TAVERN. I THOUGHT MAYBE I'D FIND SOMETHING TO DRINK,

A BUNCH OF NAZIS WERE IN THERE DOING THE SAME.

"JACOB KURTZBERG?" BIST DU JÜD? YOU ARE A JEW?!

I SAW ONE OF THEM KEPT A FANCY KNIFE IN HIS BOOT. I KEPT STARING AT IT.

DEINE MUTTER IST EINE HURE. YOUR MOTHER IS A GUTTER WHORE, BUT YOU KNOW THAT ALREADY, DON'T YOU?

DON'T TALK ABOUT MY MOTHER.

A RED SHEET FELL OVER ME. I DON'T KNOW HOW ELSE TO EXPLAIN IT.

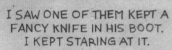

67

I TOOK THE KNIFE FROM HIS BOOT AND JUST STARTED STABBING.

DON'T TALK ABOUT MY MOTHER.

SHOTS WERE FIRED. I DON'T REMEMBER ANYTHING ELSE. AT THE END OF IT, I WAS ALIVE.

I GAVE THE KNIFE TO ROZ AS A PRESENT.

ON ANOTHER PATROL I CAME INTO A TOWN. IT WAS RECENTLY DESERTED.

A SCRAWNY GUY CAME UP TO ME. HE LOOKED LIKE A CORPSE.

ARE YOU JEWISH?

BIST DU JÜDISCH?

HE MOTIONED FOR ME TO FOLLOW HIM.

GERMANS WERE RUNNING AWAY, OFFERING SURRENDER. THEY KNEW WE WERE COMING.

HE BROUGHT ME TO A WORK CAMP.
A FACTORY.
SLAVE LABOR.

THE GERMANS RAN AWAY, SCREAMING
INSULTS ON THEIR WAY OUT.

I'D NEVER SEEN ANYTHING LIKE THIS
BEFORE. I CRIED, AND THE MAN WHO
BROUGHT ME CRIED.

OH GOD.

OH GOD.

OH GOD.

OH GOD.

THE WINTER
GOT WORSE.
FROSTBITE SET IN.

EVERY STEP WAS
SEARING PAIN.

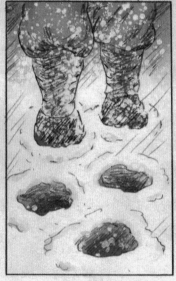

I PASSED OUT IN THE FREEZING
COLD. WHEN I WOKE UP I WAS IN
A FIELD HOSPITAL.
MY FEET WERE DEEP PURPLE.

THEY CONSIDERED AMPUTATING THEM.
LUCKY FOR ME, THEY CHOSE NOT TO.

WHILE YOU WERE UNDER,
THE PRESIDENT DIED.

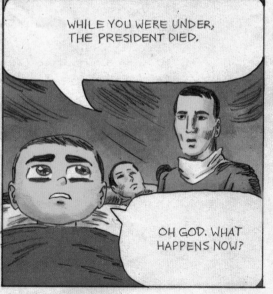

OH GOD. WHAT
HAPPENS NOW?

THEY SENT ME TO LONDON. I WASN'T GOING BACK INTO COMBAT. MY WAR WAS OVER.

ROZ GOT A LETTER FROM ME. I WASN'T ABLE TO WRITE YET, SO A NURSE TOOK DICTATION. ROZ THOUGHT MAYBE MY HANDS WERE GONE.

ONCE I GOT MY STRENGTH BACK, A C.O. APPROACHED ME.

SO I HEAR YOU'RE JACK KIRBY THE ARTIST.

GREAT! ANOTHER OFFICER WANTING HIS PORTRAIT DONE.

TURNS OUT HE WANTED ME TO MAKE DRAWINGS OF THE OTHER PATIENTS' DISEASED FEET FOR SCIENCE. I THOUGHT MINE WERE BAD. THE DOGS ON SOME OF THESE GUYS!

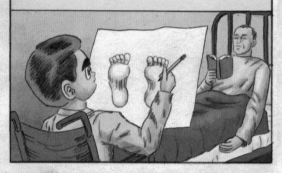

I WAS ON A BOAT WITH BRITISH COMMANDOS, BIG TOUGH GUYS WITH BIG PERSONALITIES. WE'D PLAY POKER.

ONE GAME GOT OUT OF CONTROL. A FIGHT BROKE OUT. GUYS IN WHEELCHAIRS WERE CHASING EACH OTHER.

I WAS SUPPOSED TO SAIL HOME ON THE "QUEEN MARY," BUT I GOT HELD UP, SO I ENDED UP ON A SMALL DINGHY. MY SEASICKNESS WAS OUT OF CONTROL.

I CAME HOME, BUT THEY WOULDN'T LET ME GO "HOME" HOME. I WAS AT A BASE DOWN SOUTH. CAMP BUTNER, NORTH CAROLINA.

ROZ STAYED AT A HOTEL OUTSIDE OF TOWN, BUT I WAS STRANDED, UNABLE TO GET PERMISSION TO LEAVE.

I FAKED A WEEKEND PASS WITH MY INSURANCE CARD. A PARADE OF GUYS AND THEIR GIRLS WERE LEAVING BASE.

I FLASHED MY CARD AND BLENDED IN WITH THE CROWD.

ME AND ROZ HAD OUR JOYOUS REUNION. SHE BARELY RECOGNIZED ME I WAS SO SKINNY.

A WEEK LATER THE MILITARY POLICE TRACKED US DOWN.

I WAS IN BIG TROUBLE. IT WAS DESERTION--PUNISHABLE BY DEATH.

HITLER WAS DEAD. THE NAZIS SURRENDERED.

THE WAR IN EUROPE WAS OVER.

FOUR MONTHS LATER, THE WAR IN JAPAN WAS OVER.

IN THE POSTWAR EUPHORIA THEY LET ME OFF THE HOOK. I GOT AN HONORABLE DISCHARGE AND COMMENDATIONS.

I WAS FINALLY HEADING HOME FOR REAL.

WE HAD A BABY ON THE WAY. IT WAS TIME TO GET BACK TO WORK. I PAID A VISIT TO DC COMICS PUBLISHER JACK LIEBOWITZ. HE WAS HAPPY TO SEE ME.

YOU'VE ALWAYS GOT A HOME HERE AT NATIONAL, JACK.

IT'S NOT LIKE IT USED TO BE, BUT I'LL FIND SOMETHING FOR YOU.

THEY WERE STILL USING MY STOCKPILE OF COVERS I DID BEFORE I LEFT, BUT MY ACTUAL COMICS PAGES RAN OUT AGES AGO. THEY PUT ME BACK ON BOY COMMANDOS AND SANDMAN.

IT WAS GREAT BEING BACK AT THE DRAWING BOARD. I DID A STORY ABOUT THE BOY COMMANDOS COMING HOME AFTER THE WAR.

I WOULD'VE BEEN HAPPY DOING THIS FOREVER, BUT JOE SIMON GOT DISCHARGED FROM THE COAST GUARD AND HE'D LINED UP SOME BIG PLANS FOR US.

JACK, WE'RE GOING TO WORK FOR HARVEY.

HE'D SET UP A SWEETHEART DEAL WITH HIS FORMER-ASSISTANT-TURNED-PUBLISHER AL HARVEY. ALL THE WORK WE COULD HANDLE, WITH A PIECE OF THE ACTION. WE'D GET A 50/50 SPLIT OF THE PROFITS.

JOE ALWAYS GOT US GOOD DEALS-- BETTER DEALS THAN I COULD NEGOTIATE ON MY OWN. SO I JUMPED AT THIS ONE. EDITORIAL AT NATIONAL WERE SORE THAT I DIDN'T GIVE THEM A CHANCE TO MATCH THE DEAL, SO THEY PULLED BACK ON MY WORKLOAD.

THEY SAID I WASN'T A TEAM PLAYER.

I COULDN'T COMPLAIN. CIVILIAN LIFE FELT LIKE LIVING IN LUXURY. IT WAS NICE TO BE ABLE TO GET A HAMBURGER AND CHOCOLATE CAKE WHENEVER I WANTED IT.

THE WARTIME PAPER RATIONING WAS LIFTED. COMICS WERE HEADED FOR A POSTWAR RENAISSANCE.

LITTLE BY LITTLE WE PUT THE SIMON- AND-KIRBY STUDIO BACK TOGETHER.

JOE AND I BOUGHT HOUSES ACROSS THE STREET FROM EACH OTHER ON LONG ISLAND. WE WERE NEIGHBORS.

WE CREATED A PROPOSAL FOR A NEWSPAPER COMIC STARRING INKY, A COMIC STRIP ARTIST WHO SOLVES CRIMES. IT WENT NOWHERE.

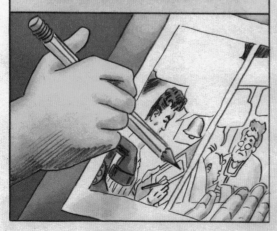

WE WROTE A PLAY, TOO. IT WAS ALONG THE LINES OF "HOW TO SUCCEED IN BUSINESS WITHOUT REALLY TRYING."

IN OUR NEW DEAL WITH HARVEY, JOE AND I DID THE BEST WORK OF OUR CAREER. STUNTMAN WAS A SMART, FUNNY SUPERHERO.

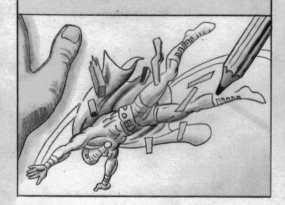

IT WAS A SCREWBALL COMEDY. IT WAS A SEND-UP AND A LOVE LETTER TO HOLLYWOOD. A STUNTMAN AND AN ACTOR WHO PLAYS DETECTIVES TEAM UP TO SOLVE CRIMES.

THE COMICS WE WERE MAKING AT THIS TIME WERE BUILT ON OUR PREVIOUS WORK. STUNTMAN WAS THE PRODUCT OF EVERYTHING WE'D LEARNED FROM YEARS OF MAKING SUPERHERO STORIES. BOY EXPLORERS WAS OUR THESIS ON THE KID GANG COMICS WE PIONEERED.

THIS IS GREAT STUFF, FELLAS!

THANKS, AL!

YOU'VE GOT GREAT TASTE!

JACK... IT'S TIME.

MR. KIRBY, IT'S A GIRL!

LITTLE SUSAN. YOU TAKE A LOOK IN YOUR BABY'S EYES AND YOU KNOW YOU GOTTA WORK HARDER THAN EVER.

WE CAN'T RUN THAT! ...IT'S AGAINST OUR POLICIES

THAT STUFF WILL NEVER BE POPULAR

IT'S A GOOD STUNT! LET'S SEE YOU DO IT

STUNTMAN

BY KIRBY NOT SIMON

HAS A BABY GIRL

WHY THE LONG FACES?

WE GOT THE SALES FIGURES BACK. THE BOOKS FLOPPED.

WE'RE GONNA HAVE TO CUT WAY BACK. I'VE GOT NOTHING FOR YOU GUYS.

THEY WERE OUR BEST EFFORTS AND BOTH COMICS TANKED. WE THOUGHT THE AVAILABILITY OF PAPER AFTER THE WAR WOULD BE GOOD FOR US.

INSTEAD IT MEANT THAT OUTFITS LIKE MARVEL COULD FLOOD THE MARKET WITH DROSS. THERE WERE TOO MANY COMICS. TOO MUCH COMPETITION. TOO MUCH JUNK. IT LOOKED LIKE THE WHOLE INDUSTRY MIGHT BE FINISHED. THERE'S A BOOM-AND-BUST CYCLE IN THE INDUSTRY, BUT WE DIDN'T KNOW THAT BACK THEN. IT WAS ALL NEW, AND THE WORST WAS YET TO COME.

ACTION SKY DARE DEVIL

FIGHTER G-MEN

I THOUGHT THE SIMON AND KIRBY REPUTATION GUARANTEED SUCCESS. I KNEW THE BOOKS WERE TOP-NOTCH. ALL OF THE SUDDEN, I HAD TIME ON MY HANDS. BARELY ANYTHING TO DO, AND A BABY GIRL COUNTING ON ME.

NOW THAT THE WAR WAS OVER, THE POPULARITY OF SUPERHEROES TOOK A NOSEDIVE. SUPERHEROES FULFILLED A WISH WE ALL HAD IN COMMON DURING THE WAR YEARS. NOW THEY SEEMED OUT OF STEP WITH THE TIMES.

COMICS WERE STARTING TO GET A BAD REPUTATION, BUT NOTHING LIKE THEY WOULD IN THE NEXT DECADE.

I HAD A PET PROJECT I PUT A LOT OF ENERGY INTO--MY SCI-FI EPIC, STARMAN ZERO. I DID A WHOLE PRESENTATION. IT WAS TOO GOOD FOR COMIC BOOKS. THIS WAS FOR THE SYNDICATES.

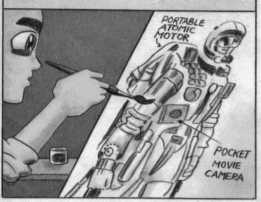

PORTABLE ATOMIC MOTOR

POCKET MOVIE CAMERA

COMIC STRIPS ARE THE WAY OUT OF THE COMIC BOOK GHETTO. BETTER PAY. PRESTIGE. A WIDER AUDIENCE, BUT NO MATTER HOW HARD I TRY, I CAN'T GET A SYNDICATE TO PICK IT UP.

READERS COMING HOME FROM THE WAR WANTED A LITTLE MORE REALISM. CRIME STORIES WERE STILL POPULAR, SO WE CAME UP WITH A NEW TWIST ON THE GENRE. WE TOOK IT TO A SMALL OUTFIT CALLED CRESTWOOD.

OUR BOOK IS CALLED "HEADLINE" COMICS. WE FIGURE THE LEAD CHARACTER SHOULD BE A REPORTER WHO WORKS THE CRIME BEAT.

'RED-HOT 'BLAZE' SPECIAL INVESTIGATOR FOR HEADLINE COMICS, KNOWS THE VALUE OF CAREFULLY-COLLECTED INFORMATION IN BRINGING A KILLER TO JUSTICE!

THEY LIKED WHAT WE DID WITH "HEADLINE." IT SOLD. WE PUT OUT MORE CRIME COMICS. THEY BECAME OUR BREAD AND BUTTER.

HILLMAN PERIODICALS WANTED US TO CREATE A COMIC IN THE VEIN OF ARCHIE, HUMOR FOR A TEENAGE AUDIENCE. WE CAME UP WITH "MY DATE." IT WAS LIGHT STUFF. JOKES. I DREW IT IN A MORE CARTOONY STYLE.

MY EMPLOYER HAS A FEW MILLION DOLLARS TO SPEND THIS EVENING AND HE WONDERS IF I MIGHT ARRANGE SOME SORT OF DATE!

HEY, SUNNY! CAN YOU LEND ME TWO BUCKS SO I CAN GET THIS CRATE FIXED? AND THEN YOU CAN BE MY DATE!!

I DID "LOCKJAW THE ALLIGATOR" AND "EARL THE RICH RABBIT" IN THAT STYLE, TOO.

LOCKJAW THE ALLIGATOR

MY HEART WASN'T IN IT, BUT I COULD DRAW THESE PAGES WAY FASTER THAN THE MUCH MORE INTERESTING CRIME BOOKS.

YOU MAY TURN IT OFF, JEEPERS.

HOW DO I LOOK? DO I MAKE A CONVINCING GANGSTER?

WE'LL SEE IF THIS GIMMICK IS ANY FASTER THAN DRAWING A COVER.

YOU LOOK LIKE EDWARD G. ROBINSON.

I ALWAYS SAW MYSELF MORE AS A JIMMY CAGNEY OR A JOHN GARFIELD.

WE DID A PHOTO SHOOT FOR OUR COVER TO MAKE IT LOOK LIKE A MAGAZINE.

ROZ PLAYED THE DAMSEL IN DISTRESS.

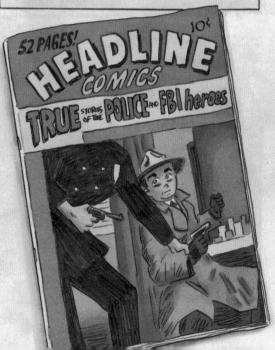

52 PAGES! 10¢ HEADLINE COMICS TRUE STORIES of the POLICE and FBI heroes

THE GUNS CAME FROM A PILE OF TOYS WE KEPT ON HAND FOR DRAWING REFERENCE. YOU CAN'T ALWAYS COUNT ON YOUR IMAGINATION. SOMETIMES WE'D EVEN USE JOE'S HUNTING RIFLE.

I HAD BOXES OF SCI-FI PAPERBACKS GOING BACK TO WHEN I WAS A KID. I HAD BOUND COPIES OF OLD COMIC STRIPS LIKE PRINCE VALIANT. YOU NEVER KNOW WHEN YOU'LL NEED INSPIRATION, OR TO INSTRUCT THE GUYS WORKING FOR US.

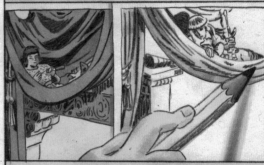

OUR STUDIO IN JOE'S ATTIC WAS GROWING.

WE HAD BEN ODA WORKING FOR US. HE WAS A PARATROOPER WHO GOT INTO THE COMICS BUSINESS AFTER THE WAR.

HOWARD FERGUSON HAD BEEN LETTERING OUR BOOKS SINCE THE CAPTAIN AMERICA DAYS. HE WAS AN IMPORTANT PART OF THE S-AND-K LOOK. HE WAS A GRUFF OLD GERMAN GUY AND SOME OF THE YOUNG ARTISTS WERE INTIMIDATED BY HIM.

DON'T MIND HIM. HE'S ALL RIGHT.

BILL DRAUT WAS MY RIGHT-HAND MAN, A PENCILLER WITH A GREAT IMAGINATION.

THERE WAS ALSO A QUIET ARTIST NAMED STEVE DITKO WHO GOT HIS START IN OUR STUDIO.

YOUR WORK IS GREAT, JACK, BUT IF YOU'RE GONNA WORK IN THIS BUSINESS YOU GOTTA PICK UP THE PACE.

I'M GONNA LET YOU IN ON A LITTLE SECRET.

I STOPPED USING THE ERASER YEARS AGO.

THE KID'S NAME WAS JACK KATZ. I HAD TO FIRE HIM FOR BEING TOO SLOW. DECADES LATER HE DREW AND SELF-PUBLISHED THE MOST DETAILED COMIC I'D EVER SEEN, "THE FIRST KINGDOM."

I'M A BIG FAN OF MILTON CANIFF'S "TERRY AND THE PIRATES." I DID MY VERSION WITH "FLYING FOOL."

EVERY DAY, WALKING PAST THE NEWS-STAND, WE'D SEE THE TRUE ROMANCE MAGAZINES. WE DECIDED TO CREATE A COMIC BOOK VERSION.

IT WAS DIFFERENT. WE DID IT OUR WAY. IT WAS QUALITY WORK, BUT WE'D FAILED RECENTLY WITH OUR BEST EFFORTS. WE DID IT ON SPEC, BETWEEN REGULAR ASSIGNMENTS. I PENCILLED 2/3 OF IT. BILL DRAUT PENCILLED THE OTHER 1/3. HOWARD FERGUSON DID THE LETTERING. JOE DID THE INKING. WE CALLED IT "YOUNG ROMANCE."

CRESTWOOD BOUGHT IT. THEY GAVE US THE DEAL WE WANTED, A 50% CUT AND WE RETAINED THE COPYRIGHT. SOMETHING ABOUT IT STRUCK A CHORD. IT WAS A MASSIVE HIT.

THE WHOLE INDUSTRY COPIED US AND WE COPIED OURSELVES WITH "YOUNG LOVE." ROMANCE SAVED THE COMIC BOOK INDUSTRY.

WE LOST A KEY MEMBER OF THE STUDIO WHEN HOWARD FERGUSON DIED SUDDENLY. SIMON AND KIRBY WASN'T THE SAME WITHOUT HIS DYNAMIC LETTERING.

WE GAVE JOHN SEVERIN AND WILL ELDER THEIR FIRST JOB IN COMICS. JOHN PENCILLED AND WILL INKED.

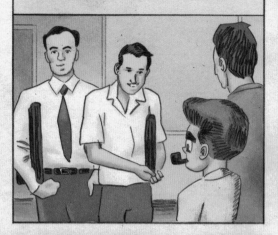

THEY DID A STORY FOR "HEADLINE COMICS" #32, "THE CLUE OF THE HOROSCOPE." AFTER THAT WE GAVE THEM WESTERNS TO WORK ON. JOHN REALLY TOOK TO THEM.

THE FAMILY KEPT GROWING. NEAL KIRBY WAS BORN. A BOY! TWO KIDS ARE EXPONENTIALLY MORE DIFFICULT THAN ONE.

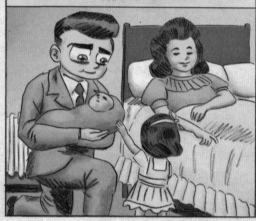

THIS IS A STRONG PORTFOLIO, CARMINE. YOU DRAW JUST LIKE ME, BUT MORE SO.

YOU KNOW, MR. KIRBY, I'M A BIG FAN OF YOU AND MR. SIMON.

LOOK, JOE. THIS INFANTINO KID IS THE REAL THING. HE DREW THE HELL OUTTA THIS. WE'LL PROBABLY END UP WORKING FOR HIM ONE DAY.

CAPTAIN AMERICA AND BUCKY

HEY, JACK. LOOK WHO THEY DUG UP OVER AT TIMELY. CAPTAIN AMERICA'S BACK. OUR BABY.

WHAT IS THIS? IT'S GARBAGE. THE WORLD'S CHANGED, BUT THEY'RE DOING CAP THE SAME OLD WAY.

LET'S SHOW THEM HOW IT'S DONE...HOW TO DO CAPTAIN AMERICA FOR THE FIFTIES.

I WAS THINKING THE SAME THING, JACK.

WE GRABBED SOME CONCEPTS FROM STARMAN ZERO. A BODY SWAP GIMMICK.

WE CREATED FIGHTING AMERICAN TO SHOW THAT WE WERE WHAT MADE CAPTAIN AMERICA GREAT. WITHOUT US HE WAS A HOLLOW SHELL. WE CREATED A SUPER POWERED EMBODIMENT OF AMERICA IN THE FIFTIES.

SORRY TO SPOIL YOUR AIM!

IT STARTED AS A STRAIGHTFORWARD SUPERHERO BOOK.

BUT THE CLICHES OF THE WAR ERA DIDN'T FLY IN THE MODERN AGE.

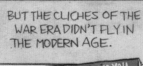

WE ADAPTED. FIGHTING AMERICAN BECAME A SATIRE.

NEXT CAME THE REAL GUT PUNCH. MY FATHER, BENJAMIN KURTZBERG, WHO I THOUGHT WAS INVINCIBLE, DIED OF HEART FAILURE. I KNOW IT WAS THE SWEATSHOPS THAT DID IT TO HIM. THEY ROBBED HIM OF HIS DIGNITY. HE SLOWLY LOST HIS SWAGGER. IT TOOK YEARS OFF HIS LIFE. IT CRUSHED HIS SPIRIT. HE WAS MY HERO, BUT I DIDN'T WANT TO END UP LIKE HIM.

MY DAUGHTER BARBARA WAS BORN. THE "B" IN BARBARA CAME FROM THE "B" FOR MY FATHER BENJAMIN.

. LIKE ALWAYS, I THREW MYSELF INTO MY WORK. THERE WERE ALWAYS COMICS THAT NEEDED DRAWING.

THE BUSINESS WAS IN TROUBLE AGAIN THANKS TO THE MIRACLE OF TELEVISION. MOVING PICTURES IN THE HOME. COWBOYS, SPACESHIPS, AND MONSTERS. WE HAD TO WORK THAT MUCH HARDER TO COMPETE.

. WESTERNS TOOK OVER TV. THEN THEY TOOK OVER COMICS. WE DID OUR S AND K VERSION OF THE WESTERN, "BOY'S RANCH," A NEW HEIGHT FOR US. MAYBE THE GREATEST COMIC WE EVER MADE TOGETHER.

IT WAS A KID GANG IN THE WILD WEST. THE BOOK WAS A GREAT PACKAGE, DOWN TO THE LAST DETAIL. WE HAD PAGES WHERE WE TAUGHT KIDS HOW TO BE COWBOYS, LIKE HOW TO TIE A LASSO.

WE PUT A LOT OF HEART INTO THAT BOOK.

DELILAH!

HA-HA-HA—

IT WAS ANOTHER FLOP, CANCELED AFTER FOUR ISSUES.

HORROR WAS HAVING A RESURGENCE. WILLIAM GAINES JR. WAS HAVING TREMENDOUS SUCCESS WITH BLOOD AND GUTS.

TERROR

EC "TALES" EC FROM THE CRYPT

FEATURING

IN THIS ISSUE: E.C.'S ADAPTATION OF A STORY BY RAY BRADBURY AMERICA'S TOP HORROR WRITER!

WAX

I WASN'T A FAN OF GORE. I'D SEEN ENOUGH OF THAT IN THE WAR. MAYBE MY HORROR BOOKS WEREN'T AS POPULAR, BUT I DID THEM ON MY TERMS.

YOUNG STEVE DITKO REALLY EXCELLED ON THE HORROR BOOKS. HE CREATED AN ATMOSPHERE AND MYSTERY. WEIRD, BUT WITHIN THE BOUNDS OF GOOD TASTE.

3-D WAS A GIMMICK THAT WENT WITH MONSTER MOVIES. IT WAS THE FLAVOR OF THE MONTH, SO WE DID 3-D COMICS. CREATING AN ILLUSION OF DEPTH WAS ALREADY PART OF MY STYLE. THIS WAS A CHANCE TO PUSH THAT FURTHER.

DITKO HELPED US ON THAT ONE, TOO. THE PROCESS WAS MORE TROUBLE THAN IT WAS WORTH, DRAWING ON DIFFERENT SHEETS OF VELLUM. BY THE TIME THE BOOK CAME OUT, THE 3-D FAD WAS OVER.

CAN'T COME TO BED 'TIL I FINISH THIS STRIP.

IS THERE ANYTHING I CAN DO TO HELP YOU?

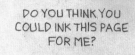

DO YOU THINK YOU COULD INK THIS PAGE FOR ME?

JUST USE A PEN TO DO THE FLAT LINES. I'LL DO THE DETAIL WORK WITH A BRUSH.

YOU KNOW I HAVE FASHION ILLUSTRATION EXPERIENCE, MR. ARTISTIC GENIUS OF THE WORLD.

DC WON THEIR ONGOING LAWSUIT AGAINST FAWCETT. THEY CLAIMED THAT CAPTAIN MARVEL WAS A RIP-OFF OF SUPERMAN. WE ALL RIPPED OFF SUPERMAN. THE BIG DIFFERENCE IS THAT CAPTAIN MARVEL OUTSOLD SUPERMAN. WE WERE CALLED IN TO TESTIFY EARLY ON SINCE WE DID ISSUE #1.

FAWCETT AGREED TO STOP PUBLISHING SUPERHEROES. THAT PUT C.C. BECK, THEIR TOP ARTIST, OUT OF WORK. HE CAME TO US ASKING FOR A SUPERHERO HE COULD WORK ON.

FIGHTING AMERICAN BIT THE DUST. WE WEREN'T REALLY DOING SUPERHEROES ANY MORE. IT SEEMED LIKE A DYING GENRE.

WE CAME UP WITH A CONCEPT CALLED "SPIDERMAN."

WE GAVE BECK A LOGO, SOME SKETCHES, AND PLOT IDEAS. WE PAIRED HIM UP WITH THE WRITER JACK OLECK. THEY REJIGGERED THE CONCEPT INTO "THE SILVER SPIDER."

NOTHING EVER HAPPENED WITH IT, SO IT ENDED UP IN A DRAWER. COMICS WAS A SINKING SHIP, AND SUPERHEROES WERE SINKING FASTER.

PUBLISHERS WERE GOING OUT OF BUSINESS. WE HAD THE BRILLIANT IDEA TO START OUR OWN PUBLISHING COMPANY, MAINLINE PUBLICATIONS. WE DID WHAT WE KNEW. ROMANCE, COWBOYS, AND CRIME. WE HAD A SUPERHERO, NIGHT FIGHTER, BUT ABANDONED IT AT THE LAST MINUTE.

WE REPLACED NIGHT FIGHTER WITH A WAR BOOK, CALLED FOXHOLE. LIKE THE ROMANCE BOOKS, WE TRIED TO MAKE IT REALISTIC. I TOLD MY STORIES. IT DIDN'T PULL ANY PUNCHES. I TURNED THE WORST MOMENTS OF MY LIFE INTO ENTERTAINMENT. WE WERE IN BUSINESS FOR OURSELVES. WE'D REACHED THE TOP OF THE COMICS FIELD.

THEN ALONG CAME DR. FREDRIC WERTHAM. THE COMICS KILLER.

HE WROTE A BOOK CALLED *SEDUCTION OF THE INNOCENT* THAT BASICALLY SAID COMIC BOOKS TURNED KIDS INTO DEVIANTS. COMICS ALREADY HAD A REPUTATION, BUT THIS WAS GASOLINE ON THE FIRE.

PARENT GROUPS ATE IT UP. IT GREW INTO A NATIONAL HYSTERIA. KIDS AND PARENTS BURNED THEIR COMICS IN PUBLIC BONFIRES.

SOON THEY WERE GOING TO HAVE SENATE HEARINGS.

WE DON'T GOT NOTHING TO WORRY ABOUT, JOE. WE DON'T DO ANY OF THAT SICK SHIT. OUR COMICS ARE WHOLESOME, GOOD CLEAN ENTERTAINMENT.

I KNOW. I KNOW.

THE SENATE KEFAUVER HEARINGS CAME. COMICS WERE ON TRIAL, AND IT WAS TELEVISED.

THERE'S BILL GAINES. I USED TO WORK FOR HIS OLD MAN.

I'M THE FIRST PUBLISHER OF HORROR COMICS IN THESE UNITED STATES. I'M RESPONSIBLE. I STARTED THEM. SOME MAY NOT LIKE THEM.

I ALWAYS THOUGHT THIS GUY WAS ASKING FOR TROUBLE.

ARE YOU WORRIED, JACK?

IT'D BE JUST AS DIFFICULT TO EXPLAIN THE HARMLESS THRILL OF A HORROR STORY TO A DOCTOR WERTHAM...

NO, MY COMICS ARE NOTHING LIKE HIS. HE WENT LOOKING FOR CONTROVERSY AND IT FOUND HIM. NOT ME. I WANT THE QUIET LIFE. YOU'LL NEVER SEE ME UP THERE.

...AS IT WOULD BE TO EXPLAIN THE SUBLIMITY OF LOVE TO A FRIGID OLD MAID.

WE HAVE PREPARED A NUMBER OF SLIDES WHICH SHOW PICTURES TAKEN FROM COMIC BOOKS. THE FIRST SUCH CRIME COMIC IS CALLED "BLACK MAGIC." YOU WILL NOTE THIS SHOWS A SANITARIUM FOR FREAKS.

BLACK MAGIC
TRUE AMAZING ACCOUNTS OF THE STRANGEST STORIES EVER TOLD!

THAT'S ME! THAT'S MY COMIC! HOW'D I GET MIXED UP IN THIS?

I CAN'T BELIEVE IT!

FREAK

THE HEARINGS THEMSELVES NEVER AMOUNTED TO ANYTHING. NO GOVERNMENT ACTION WAS TAKEN, BUT THE DAMAGE WAS DONE. THE COMICS INDUSTRY WAS IN THE TOILET. THE MAJOR PUBLISHERS GOT TOGETHER AND CAME UP WITH A COMPROMISE.

APPROVED BY THE COMICS CODE AUTHORITY

THE COMICS INDUSTRY STARTED A GROUP TO CENSOR THEMSELVES. SOME OF THE RULES SEEMED MADE TO SINGLE OUT BILL GAINES AND HIS "TALES FROM THE CRYPT."

(1) NO COMIC MAGAZINE SHALL USE THE WORD HORROR OR TERROR IN ITS TITLE.
(2) ALL SCENES OF HORROR, EXCESSIVE BLOODSHED, GORY OR GRUESOME CRIMES, DEPRAVITY, LUST, SADISM, MASOCHISM SHALL NOT BE PERMITTED.
(3) ALL LURID, UNSAVORY, GRUESOME ILLUSTRATIONS SHALL BE ELIMINATED.
(4) INCLUSION OF STORIES DEALING WITH EVIL SHALL BE USED OR SHALL BE PUBLISHED ONLY WHERE THE INTENT IS TO ILLUSTRATE A MORAL ISSUE AND IN NO CASE SHALL EVIL BE PRESENTED ALLURINGLY, NOR SO AS TO INJURE THE SENSIBILITIES OF THE READER.
(5) SCENES DEALING WITH, OR INSTRUMENTS ASSOCIATED WITH WALKING DEAD, TORTURE, VAMPIRES AND VAMPIRISM, GHOULS, CANNIBALISM, AND WEREWOLFISM ARE PROHIBITED.

PARENT GROUPS TARGETED THE COMICS INDUSTRY JUST LONG ENOUGH TO CUT ITS LEGS OUT FROM UNDER IT. THEN THEY MOVED ON TO TARGET THE NEXT THING TO COME ALONG, ROCK 'N' ROLL.

THE INDUSTRY'S DEATH WAS ACCELERATED. PUBLISHERS WERE GETTING DESPERATE. CRESTWOOD, WHO WE DID "YOUNG ROMANCE" AND "JUSTICE TRAPS THE GUILTY" FOR, CUT WAY BACK ON OUR WORK BECAUSE OF OUR SELF-PUBLISHED "MAINLINE" BOOKS.

YOU'RE DOING ROMANCE AND CRIME FOR US AND YOU'RE DOING A COMPETING VERSION FOR YOURSELF? YOU THINK I DON'T KNOW WHAT THIS MEANS?

IT MEANS I'M PAYING YOU FOR THE CRAP WHILE YOU SAVE THE GOOD STUFF FOR YOURSELF.

WHO NEEDS THEM, ANYWAY. WE'VE GOT OUR OWN BOOKS. WE CAN PUT EVEN MORE TIME AND EFFORT INTO THEM, JOE.

LEADER NEWS WAS OUR DISTRIBUTOR. THEY GOT OUR BOOKS TO THE NEWSSTAND. THEY ALSO DISTRIBUTED BILL GAINES'S EC COMICS. IT WAS A BIG PART OF THEIR BUSINESS. ALL OF THE SUDDEN, STORES REFUSED TO CARRY THE EC BOOKS, EVEN AFTER THEY COMPLIED WITH THE NEW COMICS CODE.

THE BACKLASH AND BOYCOTTS AGAINST "TALES FROM THE CRYPT" AND THOSE BOOKS HIT OUR DISTRIBUTOR HARD. EVEN AFTER GAINES TONED DOWN HIS COMICS AND COMPLIED WITH THE NEW COMICS CODE, THE DAMAGE WAS ALREADY DONE. CRATES OF BOOKS CAME BACK TO THE DISTRIBUTOR UNOPENED, OURS INCLUDED.

BAD NEWS, JACK. OUR DISTRIBUTOR IS OUT OF BUSINESS.

BUT WHAT HAPPENS TO ALL THE MONEY THEY OWE US?

ME AND JOE HAD TO SHUT IT ALL DOWN. WE SOLD THE COMPANY TO A DOWN AND DIRTY OUTFIT IN CONNECTICUT CALLED CHARLTON COMICS.

SORRY, FELLAS. WE'RE CLOSING THE STUDIO. IT'S OVER.

SAY IT AIN'T SO!

IT WAS HARD LAYING THOSE GUYS OFF, BUT THE HARDEST PART WAS ENDING ME AND JOE'S PARTNERSHIP AFTER ALMOST 20 YEARS.

WE'D BEEN PARTNERS FOR ALMOST AS LONG AS I'D BEEN IN THE BUSINESS.

SIMON AND KIRBY WAS KAPUT. IT WAS JUST BUSINESS--NOTHING PERSONAL. THE YEARS HAD WORN AWAY AT THE WARMTH OF OUR FRIENDSHIP. BY THE END WE WERE BUSINESS PARTNERS, BUT NOT THAT MUCH MORE. NOW WE WEREN'T EVEN THAT.

I NEEDED A JOB. I WENT LOOKING FOR WORK AT NATIONAL, BETTER KNOWN AS DC COMICS. JACK SCHIFF WAS HAPPY TO SEE ME.

YOU DIDN'T NEED TO BRING YOUR PORTFOLIO, JACK. I'M A FAN. YOUR WORK IS ALWAYS STELLAR.

HE GAVE ME ASSIGNMENTS THAT CAME NATURALLY TO ME--SCIENCE FICTION STORIES:

HOUSE of SECRETS

TALES OF THE UNEXPECTED

GREATEST ADVENTURE

HOUSE of MYSTERY

BAH! IT'S HOPELESS! THERE IS NOTHING WE CAN DO FOR HIM!

THE MAN WHO COLLECTED PLANETS

IT WAS A LITTLE BIT LONELY NOT SHARING A STUDIO WITH JOE AND THE GUYS. I WAS WORKING EXCLUSIVELY IN MY BASEMENT. WHILE ROZ AND THE KIDS SLEPT, I MAINLY HAD MYSELF TO TALK TO.

THE FOOL HAS SIDED WITH THE EARTHMAN! STOP THEM!

IT WAS WORK, BUT IT WASN'T THE WORKLOAD I WAS ACCUSTOMED TO. IT WAS TOUGH GOING FROM CALLING YOUR OWN SHOTS, TO ANSWERING TO AN EDITOR.

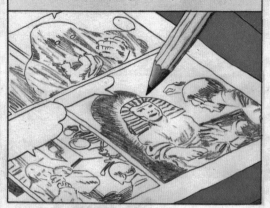

WHENEVER I NEEDED AN IDEA, I'D RUMMAGE THROUGH MY PULP COLLECTION UNTIL SOMETHING JUMPED OUT AT ME.

EVERY STORY NEEDED A UNIQUE GIMMICK TO SET IT APART. WE WERE SELLING NOVELTY.

WHAT ARE YOU DOING, DADDY?

I'M JUST LOOKING AT SOME OLD SCIENCE FICTION BOOKS, LOOKING FOR INSPIRATION.

HMMM...

BULLFINCH'S MYTHOLOGY

IT WASN'T JUST SCI-FI. I TOOK EQUAL INSPIRATION FROM HISTORY AND MYTHOLOGY.

I DID A STORY ABOUT A GUY WHO FOUND THOR'S MAGICAL HAMMER, MJOLNIR.

THIS IS A TRICK TO STEAL MY HAMMER, BUT YOU WON'T!

JACK, YOU'RE REALLY COOKING! I WISH I HAD TEN OF YOU.

I'VE GOT TIME FOR MORE ASSIGNMENTS. I CAN HANDLE A MUCH BIGGER WORKLOAD.

I LIKE DOING THESE SHORT STORIES, BUT I'D REALLY LIKE TO DO SOMETHING LONGER WITH RECURRING CHARACTERS.

SOUNDS INTERESTING.

WE HAD A BUNCH OF UNUSED AND UNFINISHED CONCEPTS FROM THE SIMON AND KIRBY DAYS. JOE SAID I COULD DO WHATEVER I NEEDED TO WITH OUR JOINT WORKS-IN-PROGRESS. I FOUND ONE, BUT I WANTED TO DOUBLE-CHECK WITH JOE JUST TO BE SURE.

JOE, I WANT TO DO SOMETHING WITH THAT "CHALLENGERS OF THE UNKNOWN" CONCEPT.

JACK, I TOLD YOU, YOU HAVE MY BLESSING. THAT STUFF IS ANCIENT HISTORY. I'VE MOVED ON. IF YOU THINK YOU CAN MAKE "CHALLENGERS OF THE UNKNOWN" FLY IN THIS HOSTILE MARKET, GO FOR IT.

THEY WERE A TEAM OF FOUR ADVENTURERS, EACH THE TOP IN THEIR FIELD, WHO WERE IN A PLANE CRASH. THEY REALIZED THEY SHOULD'VE DIED AND THAT THEY WERE LIVING ON BORROWED TIME, SO THEY SWORE AN OATH TO MAKE THE MOST OF LIFE, FACING IMPOSSIBLE ODDS.

DC HAD THEIR WAY OF DOING THINGS. JACK SCHIFF TEAMED ME UP WITH THE WRITER DAVE WOOD ON THE SCRIPTS FOR "CHALLENGERS," EVEN THOUGH I DID MOST OF THE WRITING.

JACK SCHIFF PUT ME ON GREEN ARROW, AGAIN WITH WRITER DAVE WOOD. I'D WORKED ON ARCHERS BEFORE, LIKE BULLSEYE. GREEN ARROW WAS A BATMAN RIP-OFF.

I WANTED TO REALLY TURN IT INTO SOMETHING--BUILD IT FROM THE GROUND UP, BUT THEY WOULDN'T LET ME MAKE ANY BIG CHANGES.

MORT WEISINGER NO LONGER EDITED GREEN ARROW, BUT HE CREATED THE CHARACTER SO HE HAD SOME SAY IN IT.

JACK, REMEMBER...GREEN ARROW IS MY BABY. TRY NOT TO TURN IT INTO COMPLETE AND UTTER CRAP, OKAY?

MORT WASN'T A FAN, AND HE MADE SURE I DIDN'T DO MY OWN THING WITH IT. I DID MANAGE TO CREATE AN ORIGIN FOR GREEN ARROW, A RIFF ON ROBINSON CRUSOE.

I WAS DOING COMIC BOOKS, BECAUSE IT'S WHAT I KNEW. IT'S WHAT I'M GOOD AT, BUT I WAS LOOKING FOR OTHER VENUES. WHO KNEW HOW MUCH LONGER THE INDUSTRY WOULD LAST? I STARTED PUTTING TOGETHER SOME MORE COMIC STRIP IDEAS.

I ENLISTED HELP FROM MY FRIENDS AND FORMER STUDIOMATES. I SENT THEM AROUND TO THE SYNDICATES.

ONE CONCEPT WAS "SURF HUNTER," AN UNDERSEA EXPLORER. I WAS TRYING TO TAKE ADVANTAGE OF THE SKIN-DIVING TREND.

I GOT IN TOUCH WITH WALLY WOOD TO POSSIBLY INK IT.

I COLLABORATED ON A SCI-FI COMIC STRIP WITH DAVE WOOD, NO RELATION TO WALLY. IT WAS G-MEN IN SPACE. WE CALLED IT "SPACE BUSTERS."

I HAD ANOTHER COMIC STRIP IDEA. I CALLED JOHN SEVERIN TO SEE IF HE WANTED TO WORK ON IT WITH ME.

IT'S ABOUT A CIGAR-CHEWING ARMY SERGEANT AND HIS UNIT OF MISFIT G.I.S.

GEE, JACK. I'LL HAVE TO THINK ABOUT IT.

IT WAS A GROWN-UP VERSION OF THE BOY COMMANDOS. JOHN PASSED ON THE IDEA, SO I SAVED IT FOR LATER.

I TRIED EVERYTHING. I DID A SAMPLE STRIP CALLED "ON THE GREEN WITH PETER PARR." IT WAS A COMIC ABOUT THE LIFE OF A PROFESSIONAL GOLFER. IT WAS REJECTED.

I DID ONE ABOUT A JAZZ MUSICIAN CALLED "KING MASTERS." I NEVER HEARD BACK FROM THE SYNDICATES ON THIS ONE EITHER.

UNLATCH FROM THAT HORN MAN! I GOTTA MAKE MY PITCH BEFORE THE BOSS GIVES US THE DOWNBEAT FOR REHEARSAL

RING RING

HEY, JOHN! DID YOU CHANGE YOUR MIND ABOUT THE ARMY COMIC?

JOHN? NO, THIS IS JOE. JOE SIMON. AND NOBODY BUYS WAR COMICS. YOU KNOW THAT.

SO JACK, DO YOU WANT TO DO SOME MORE COMICS WITH ME FOR AL HARVEY? I'M MISSING COMICS A LOT MORE THAN I THOUGHT I WOULD. I WAS THINKING MAYBE WE COULD DO SOME SCI-FI STORIES.

WE DID A BOOK CALLED "ALARMING TALES." IT FEATURED:

MINIATURE CLONES

INTERDIMENSIONAL TRAVEL

A CHAIR THAT FLIES THROUGH SPACE

POSTAPOCALYPTIC TALKING ANIMALS

WE DID "RACE FOR THE MOON," WHICH USED CONCEPTS SIMILAR TO WHAT I WAS DOING IN "SPACE BUSTERS."

THE FACE ON MARS

IN THE MEANTIME, I PUT TOGETHER ANOTHER COMIC STRIP PROPOSAL, "KAMANDI OF THE CAVES." LIKE THE OTHERS, IT WENT NOWHERE. ALL THESE COMICS I WAS SENDING TO THE SYNDICATES WERE ADDING UP TO NOTHING.

JACK SCHIFF HAD SOME NEWS.

I HAVE A FRIEND AT THE GEORGE MATTHEW ADAMS SERVICE. HE'S LOOKING FOR A COMIC STRIP ABOUT SPACE. HE ASKED ME TO HELP HIM FIND ONE.

DO YOU HAVE ANYTHING LIKE THAT?

I BROUGHT IN SPACE BUSTERS.

I SHOWED THIS TO MY FRIEND AT THE SYNDICATE. HE SAID HE WANTS SOMETHING LESS FANTASTICAL. HE WANTS MORE PULLED-FROM-THE-HEADLINES SPACE RACE STUFF.

DAVE WOOD AND I PLAYED AROUND WITH POSSIBLE NAMES FOR THE STRIP.

WE SETTLED ON "SKY MASTERS."

WITH THE COLLAPSE OF EC COMICS, WALLY WOOD MOVED OUT OF COMIC BOOKS AND INTO ILLUSTRATION.

HE AGREED TO INK "SKY MASTERS." HE WAS EXCITED TO HAVE HIS WORK IN NEWSPAPERS. HE WAS A FAN OF MY WORK, AND I WAS A FAN OF HIS.

JACK, I WANT YOU TO SIGN THIS. DAVE WOOD HAS ALREADY SIGNED IT. I JUST NEED YOURS.

FOUR PERCENT? I DON'T KNOW.

HE DIDN'T OUT-AND-OUT THREATEN TO TAKE AWAY ASSIGNMENTS, BUT HIS GESTURES WERE VERY ELOQUENT.

IF YOU DON'T SIGN THIS I WOULD THINK ILL OF YOU, JACK.

I'D BE VERY... UNHAPPY.

MAYBE YOU'RE NOT THE KIND OF MAN I THINK YOU ARE.

IT SEEMED TO ME MY LIVELIHOOD WAS BEING THREATENED.

SIGN IT.

SO I DID. I COULDN'T AFFORD TO ALIENATE MY MAIN SOURCE OF WORK.

I FIGURED ONCE THE STRIP WAS A SUCCESS, I COULD FIGURE SOMETHING OUT. I HAD WORK TO DO.

I STROVE FOR ACCURACY, BUT MOSTLY I WAS MAKING UP WHAT I THOUGHT REAL WORLD SPACE TRAVEL WOULD BE. I HAD MY PULP COLLECTION AND SUBSCRIPTION TO POPULAR MECHANICS TO HELP ME.

AFTER RUSSIA LAUNCHED SPUTNIK, THE COUNTRY WENT SPACE CRAZY. ROCKET LAUNCHES WERE BIG NEWS.

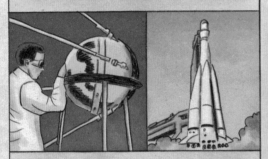

AMERICA WAS IN A SPACE RACE AND WE WERE COMING IN SECOND. THE STRIP WAS DOING WELL. IT STRUCK A CHORD, BUT I WAS LOSING MY SHIRT.

IT DIDN'T TAKE THEM LONG TO FIGURE OUT THAT I WAS ON THE UP-AND-UP.

I WAS HAVING TROUBLE WITH THE COMIC. DAVE WOOD WAS LATE WITH HIS SCRIPTS. HE WAS HOLDING UP THE PROCESS SO I WROTE THE DIALOGUE MYSELF.

DAVE WOOD AND I SPLIT THE MONEY FROM THE SYNDICATE 50/50. I WAS PAYING WALLY WOOD AND JACK SCHIFF OUT OF POCKET. I HAD MY DREAM OF BEING A REAL SYNDICATED CARTOONIST AND I WAS LOSING MONEY.

I GOT A VISIT FROM THE F.B.I.

REGARDING THE TECHNOLOGY YOU DEPICT IN YOUR CARTOONS...WHERE DID YOU HEAR ABOUT THIS TECHNOLOGY.

I DUNNO...I JUST MADE IT UP.

I WAS ALREADY COMING UP WITH THE PLOTS AND WRITING FIRST DRAFT DIALOGUE, SO FILLING IN THE BALLOONS WAS NO HARDSHIP. IT JUST GALLED ME TO HAVE DEAD WEIGHT HOLDING ME DOWN.

AT LAST I'VE WON! ONCE I'VE LINED UP DIRECTION AND TURNED ON FULL THROTTLE...

...MAN'S FIRST HOME IN SPACE WILL BE BLASTED FROM THE UNIVE...

I FINALLY GOT HOLD OF DAVE WOOD.

LOOK, DAVE. I'M DOING ALL THE WORK ON THIS AND I'M NOT GETTING A DIME. I'M PAYING SCHIFF HIS FINDER'S FEE AND I'M PAYING WALLY FOR THE INKS AND LETTERING. THIS 50/50 SPLIT ISN'T WORKING AND IT ISN'T FAIR.

WELL, JACK, MY BROTHER HELPS ME WITH THE WRITING, SO I'VE BEEN PAYING HIM WITH MY CUT.

WE SETTLED ON A 60/40 SPLIT FOR ME.

JACK SCHIFF ASKED ME FOR AN EVEN BIGGER PERCENTAGE THAN BEFORE.

ENOUGH IS ENOUGH. NO WAY.

I STOPPED PAYING HIM. I KNEW WHAT THAT WOULD MEAN.

SCHIFF FIRED ME FROM "CHALLENGERS OF THE UNKNOWN," THE BOOK I BROUGHT TO HIM.

ARE YOU JACK KIRBY?

YEAH, WHO'S ASKING?

YOU'VE JUST BEEN SERVED.

JACK SCHIFF SUED ME OVER "SKY MASTERS." I SUED HIM RIGHT BACK.

I WAS BLACKBALLED AT DC, WHERE MOST OF MY WORK WAS COMING FROM. NOBODY THERE WOULD TOUCH ME. I HAD TO LOOK AT OTHER VENUES.

I WAS WORKING ON SKY MASTERS AND THAT WAS PRETTY MUCH IT.

THERE WAS A GLIMMER OF HOPE. SOMETHING BIG. I GOT A CALL FROM AN AGENT WHO SAW SKY MASTERS AND WANTED ME TO PITCH A SCI-FI SHOW TO CBS TELEVISION.

I WENT TO MY FILES AND GOT OUT STARMAN ZERO.

I FRESHENED IT UP AND RENAMED IT "TIGER-21." I PITCHED IT TO CBS.

CBS
TELEVISION
NETWORK

THINGS WERE LOOKING PROMISING.

I GOT ANOTHER CALL FROM JOE SIMON.

LET'S DO SOME SUPERHERO BOOKS. I THINK WE'RE DUE FOR A SUPERHERO COMEBACK.

WE RETOOLED "THE SHIELD" FOR ARCHIE COMICS. WE RENAMED IT "THE DOUBLE LIFE OF PRIVATE STRONG."

WE HAD A MINI SIMON AND KIRBY RENAISSANCE.

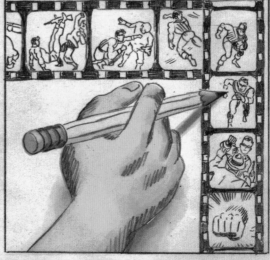

LET'S SEE IF WE CAN DO SOMETHING WITH THIS.

WE TOOK THE OLD UNFINISHED SPIDERMAN PROPOSAL AND MADE A NEW COMIC OUT OF IT.

THE ORPHAN TOMMY TROY FINDS A MIRACLE RING THAT GRANTS HIM THE POWERS OF A BUG.

C.C. BECK'S APPROACH WAS A COMEDIC FAIRY TALE WITH MAGICAL GENIES. MINE WAS BROODING SCIENCE FICTION WITH EXTRA-DIMENSIONAL INSECT PEOPLE.

CLICK

THERE WAS A POPULAR MONSTER MOVIE CALLED "THE FLY," AND THAT'S WHAT WE RECHRISTENED SPIDERMAN AS... THE FLY.

THE DAY CAME WHEN I WAS FACE TO FACE WITH JACK SCHIFF IN A COURT OF LAW.

JOE SIMON AND JACK OLECK, ONE OF OUR WRITERS FROM THE SIMON AND KIRBY DAYS, WERE THERE.

MY FRIEND, THE PRESIDENT OF DC COMICS, JACK LIEBOWITZ, GAVE TESTIMONY ON SCHIFF'S BEHALF.

THE SYNDICATE APPROACHED ME AND ASKED IF I HAD ANY IDEAS FOR SCIENCE FICTION STRIPS, SO I ASSIGNED IT TO JACK SCHIFF.

HE THREATENED TO CUT DOWN MY WORK IF I DIDN'T PLAY BALL.

DID HE TELL YOU ANY WORDS OR SUBSTANCE THAT IF YOU WOULD NOT SIGN THAT NOTE YOU WOULD NOT GET ANY MORE ASSIGNMENTS.

I'LL GIVE YOU HIS GESTURES.

I WANT HIS WORDS, NOT HIS GESTURES.

HIS GESTURES WERE VERY ELOQUENT.

YOU HAVE TO GIVE ME HIS WORDS.

HE SAID HE WOULD THINK ILL OF ME.

DID HE SAY ANYTHING BESIDES THAT?

HE SAID HE WOULD BE UNHAPPY.

ANYTHING ELSE?

"SIGN IT."

YOUR HONOR, WE FIND IN FAVOR OF THE PLAINTIFF, MR. SCHIFF.

I LOST.
THE COURT DECIDED
I'D HAVE TO PAY SCHIFF AS
LONG AS THE STRIP RAN.

SO I KILLED IT.
EVERY CARTOONIST'S DREAM...
A SYNDICATED COMIC STRIP AND
I LET IT DIE.

ME AND JOE'S SUPERHERO BOOKS
BOMBED SO NOW I WAS COMPLETELY,
UTTERLY UNEMPLOYED.

I RAN INTO JOE SIMON ON THE STREET.

IS THIS HOW A SYNDICATED CARTOONIST DRESSES?

I'LL NEVER DO ANOTHER SYNDICATED STRIP AGAIN.

I HATE GOING BACKWARD, BUT I SWALLOWED MY PRIDE AND WENT BACK TO WHERE IT ALL BEGAN.

JACK KIRBY IS HERE TO SEE YOU.

SEND HIM IN, FLO.

I WAS GOING HAT-IN-HAND TO THE OFFICE OF THE GUY I SAID I'D FUCKING KILL IF I EVER SAW HIM AGAIN. NOW I'M LOOKING FOR A JOB FROM HIM. I WAS AT THE END OF MY ROPE.

STAN LEE

APPARENTLY SO WAS HE. I CAME IN AND HE LOOKED LIKE HE'D BEEN CRYING. WORKMEN WERE CARRYING THE FURNITURE OUT.

THAT'S HOW JACK REMEMBERS IT, BUT NEITHER ONE OF US HAS A GOOD MEMORY. WHAT JACK DIDN'T TELL YOU IS IF I WAS CRYING, MAYBE IT WAS BECAUSE I'D LOST MY BEST FRIEND AND ARTISTIC COLLABORATOR JOE MANEELY TO A FREAK ACCIDENT.

AFTER JACK AND JOE LEFT BACK IN THE CAPTAIN AMERICA DAYS, I HAD TO KEEP THE SHIP RUNNING, AND IT WASN'T EASY. EVEN IN THE GOOD DAYS WHEN COMICS WERE BOOMING, MARTIN EXPECTED ME TO RUN THE COMICS DIVISION ON A SHOESTRING. MARVEL WAS THE RED-HEADED STEPCHILD OF HIS MAGAZINE EMPIRE.

PEOPLE TALK LIKE MARTIN WAS MY DEAR DOTING UNCLE, BUT THAT WASN'T THE CASE. HIS WIFE WAS MY MOM'S COUSIN. THAT GOT ME IN THE DOOR AS OFFICE BOY, BUT THE REST WAS BECAUSE I WORKED NON-STOP.

I HAD AMBITION. I WANTED TO BE A WRITER. I CAME UP WITH THE "NOM DE PLUME" STAN LEE.

AFTER MARTIN FIRED JACK AND JOE...

THINK YOU CAN RUN THIS PLACE WHILE I LOOK FOR A PERMANENT REPLACEMENT?

I DID IT ALL. IF AN ARTIST CAME LOOKING FOR WORK, I'D WRITE SOMETHING ON THE SPOT FOR THEM.

ANYTHING I DIDN'T HAVE ROOM FOR IN THE BOOKS WENT IN THE INVENTORY PILE.

SIMON AND KIRBY WERE A TOUGH ACT TO FOLLOW, BUT WE KEPT CAPTAIN AMERICA GOING WITH SYD SHORES AND JOHN ROMITA.

I WROTE A BOOK ABOUT THE PROCESS OF HOW COMICS WERE MADE.

MY MILITARY DESIGNATION WAS "PLAYWRIGHT." I WAS IN THE SIGNAL CORPS. WORD GOT OUT I WAS A "FAMOUS COMIC BOOK WRITER." I GOT TRANSFERRED TO THE TRAINING FILMS DIVISION WHERE I WROTE SCRIPTS ABOUT HEALTH AND HYGIENE. I DID CARTOONS FOR "STARS AND STRIPES."

I CONTINUED WRITING SCRIPTS FOR TIMELY/MARVEL. ONE TIME THERE WAS A LETTER FROM TIMELY WITH MY ASSIGNMENT IN IT.

I COULD SEE IT IN MY MAILBOX, BUT THE CLERK WASN'T ON DUTY, SO I UNSCREWED THE DOOR AND GOT IT.

SAY! WHAT GIVES?!

I ALMOST GOT SENT TO LEAVENWORTH FOR MY WORK ETHIC.

AFTER THE WAR, COMICS WAS A DIFFERENT FIELD. MARTIN WANTED US TO FOLLOW FADS. IT MADE SENSE TO ME. SUPERHEROES GAVE WAY TO CRIME, TO ROMANCE, TO HORROR, TO WESTERN, TO SCI-FI, TO FUNNY ANIMALS.

THINGS WERE GETTING BAD. COMICS WERE BEING VILIFIED. I KEPT SMILING, KEPT WORKING HARDER.

I DID A COMIC STRIP FOR THE SYNDICATES ABOUT A MAIL CARRIER CALLED "WILLIE LUMPKIN." I WORKED WITH DAN DECARLO ON IT.

WILLIE LUMPKIN BOMBED, BUT DAN WENT ON TO BIG SUCCESS AT ARCHIE.

I FOUND A GREAT COLLABORATOR IN THE ARTIST JOE MANEELY.

WE DID A COMIC IN THE AGE OF KING ARTHUR CALLED "BLACK KNIGHT."

YOUR PARDON, PENDRAGON! I'VE SWORN AN OATH TO REVEAL MYSELF TO NO MAN!

I HAD BIG PLANS FOR MY PARTNERSHIP WITH JOE.

I GOT WORD THAT JOE HAD DIED THE NIGHT BEFORE. HE WAS OUT LATE WITH JOHN SEVERIN AND FELL IN FRONT OF A SUBWAY CAR. I WAS DEVASTATED.

MARTIN DISCOVERED MY STOCKPILE OF UNPUBLISHED COMICS ARTWORK GOING BACK YEARS. ALL PAID FOR, BUT NEVER USED.

NO NEW ART UNTIL YOU'VE USED UP THIS BACKLOG.

COMICS HAD TURNED ME INTO AN OLD MAN.

MARTIN AND THE REST OF THE COMPANY LOOKED DOWN ON THE COMICS DIVISION. AND THAT WAS DURING THE GOOD TIMES.

THE COMICS DIVISION WAS ON LIFE SUPPORT. THEN I GOT WORD THAT AFTER 27 YEARS, MARTIN WAS SHUTTING US DOWN.

MY WIFE JOANIE TOLD ME THERE WAS AN OPPORTUNITY THERE.

IF MARTIN'S GOING TO FIRE YOU AND CLOSE THE WHOLE THING DOWN, WHY NOT DO IT YOUR WAY? MAKE THE COMICS YOUR WAY. THE WAY YOU ALWAYS TALKED ABOUT.

I DON'T REMEMBER ANY CRYING. MAYBE I WAS JUST TIRED, HEAD IN HANDS.

AND THEN JACK KIRBY WALKED IN THE DOOR.

AS IN ALL THINGS REGARDING THE MARVEL YEARS, STANLEY HAS HIS VERSION. MY VERSION IS SIMPLE. I SAVED MARVEL'S ASS.

TELL MARTIN TO HOLD OFF. WE CAN TURN THINGS AROUND. I'VE GOT A MILLION IDEAS.

I WANTED TO DO SCI-FI STORIES, SO I PUT IN SCI-FI ELEMENTS. DC OWNED THE COMPANY THAT DISTRIBUTED MARVEL'S COMICS. THEIR BREAD AND BUTTER WAS SUPERHEROES, SO THEY DIDN'T WANT MARVEL DOING ANY SUPERHEROES.

LOOK, JACK. WE GOT SOME WESTERN AND MONSTER BOOKS. I CAN FIT YOU IN THERE.

WE CAN SNEAK IN THE SUPERHEROES. LONE RANGER IS BASICALLY A SUPERHERO. WE CAN LOAD THE WESTERNS AND MONSTERS WITH THIS STUFF.

STANLEY CAME TO LIFE IN THE COURSE OF OUR TALK. WE TALKED AND TALKED. I CAME OUT OF IT ENERGIZED. IF MONSTERS AND WESTERNS WERE WHAT WE WERE DOING, WE'D MAKE THE BEST ONES POSSIBLE. IF THIS WAS THE END OF COMICS, GO OUT WITH A BANG.

WE PUT MONSTERS, ALIENS, AND SCI-FI GIMMICKS IN THE WESTERNS.

RADIOACTIVE MONSTER MOVIES WERE ALL THE RAGE. I ADDED MY OWN TWIST TO THEM. I MADE THEM SUPER.

FIN FANG FOOM

GROOT

WE DID A RECURRING SUPER-MAGICIAN CHARACTER, "THE FANTASTIC DOCTOR DROOM," IN THE MONSTER BOOKS. HE WAS LIKE MANDRAKE THE MAGICIAN.

HE FOUGHT ALIEN INVASIONS. IT DIDN'T LAST TOO LONG.

NATIONAL WAS HAVING SUCCESS WITH THEIR NEW SUPERHERO TEAM, "THE JUSTICE LEAGUE OF AMERICA."

STEVE DITKO WAS DOING MONSTER STORIES AT MARVEL, TOO, BUT HE WAS ALSO DOING A NEW SUPERHERO FOR THAT CONNECTICUT OUTFIT ME AND JOE SOLD OUR COMPANY TO.

ME AND STAN DECIDED TO GO FOR IT. WE DID A SUPERHERO BOOK, BUT WE KEPT IT DISGUISED. WE DIDN'T DARE MAKE IT FULL-ON SUPERHEROES. NO COSTUMES. WE EMPHASIZED THE MONSTERS ON THE COVER.

THEY WERE AN UPDATE OF THE CHALLENGERS OF THE UNKNOWN. WE CALLED THEM "THE FANTASTIC FOUR." BEN GRIMM WAS NAMED AFTER MY DAD. SUSAN STORM WAS NAMED AFTER MY DAUGHTER.

IT COMBINED EVERYTHING I'D EVER WORKED ON: SUPERHEROES, ROMANCE, MONSTERS, SPACE OPERA. MARVEL NEEDED A HIT. WE DIDN'T REALIZE IT WAS, AT FIRST. WE GOT AN INKLING WHEN THE LETTERS STARTED ROLLING IN.

DEAR EDITOR... THE CONTINUITY IN THE FANTASTIC FOUR IS ALL THAT COULD POSSIBLY BE ASKED.

THE MARVEL RATES WERE LOW, BUT I WAS WORKING AROUND THE CLOCK. I ALWAYS MADE TIME FOR BREAKFAST WITH THE FAMILY, INCLUDING OUR NEW ADDITION, BABY LISA.

MONSTER MOVIES WERE A CONSTANT INSPIRATION. OLD ONES RAN ON TV. NEW ONES WERE ADVERTISED

PICTURE IT, A GUY WHO, WHEN TROUBLE HITS, SUMMONS THE STRENGTH WE ALL HAVE INSIDE OF US.

I ONCE SAW A WOMAN LIFT HER CAR. HER BABY WAS CAUGHT UNDER THE RUNNING BOARD. THE LITTLE CHILD WAS PLAYING IN THE GUTTER AND WAS CRAWLING ONTO THE SIDEWALK UNDER THE RUNNING BOARD OF THIS CAR.

IN DESPERATION HIS MOTHER LIFTED THE REAR END OF THE CAR. IT SUDDENLY CAME TO ME THAT IN DESPERATION WE ALL DO THAT. I'VE DONE IT MYSELF. I'VE BENT STEEL.

I'VE ALWAYS LIKED THE WORD "HULK."

I DID A COMBO OF "THE BEAST OF THE YUCCA FLATS," "FRANKENSTEIN," "DR. JEKYLL AND MR. HYDE," AND THE PATHOS OF "THE WOLFMAN."

"THE HULK" WAS A MODERN MONSTER, CAUSED BY GAMMA RADIATION.

LIKE THE WOLFMAN, HE WAS A TORTURED SOUL, AND CHANGED IN THE FULL MOON.

THE ALL-NIGHTERS CONTINUED, THEN BREAKFAST WITH THE FAMILY, THEN BED.

I'D WAKE UP IN TIME FOR DINNER, THEN BACK TO WORK UNTIL BREAKFAST AGAIN.

ONCE OR TWICE A WEEK I'D GO INTO THE CITY TO TURN IN MY WORK AND HAVE STORY CONFERENCES WITH STANLEY.

THIS IS JACK KIRBY.

OH, HI!

JUDY GARLAND!

MARIE SEVERIN.

SOL BRODSKY RAN PRODUCTION. MARIE DID COLOR AND CORRECTIONS FOR HIM-- WHATEVER GOT THE BOOKS OUT THE DOOR. WITHIN A FEW YEARS SHE WAS A COMICS STAR IN HER OWN RIGHT.

TV AND THE RADIO WERE MY COMPANIONS THROUGH THE LONG WORKNIGHT.

TONIGHT ON THE LATE SHOW...THE INCREDIBLE SHRINKING MAN.

WE DID A RIFF ON THE INCREDIBLE SHRINKING MAN CALLED "THE MAN IN THE ANT HILL" ABOUT HENRY PYM AND HIS SHRINKING SERUM.

A FEW MONTHS LATER WE BROUGHT HIM BACK WITH A FULL SUPERHERO MAKEOVER AS ANT-MAN.

I'VE ALWAYS BEEN INTERESTED IN MYTHOLOGY. I'D DONE A BUNCH OF COMICS ABOUT THOR. I LIKE THE IDEA OF UPDATING THE OLD STORIES.

ONE OF MY FIRST COMICS WAS ABOUT THE SON OF THOR AND A NEW GENERATION OF GODS FOR OUR MODERN ERA. I SUGGESTED TO STAN THAT WE DO THOR AS A SUPERHERO, WITH A LITTLE BIT OF SUPERMAN AND CAPTAIN MARVEL THROWN IN.

HE HAD A DUAL IDENTITY, DON BLAKE, A LAME SURGEON HE'D TRADE PLACES WITH, LIKE FREDDIE FREEMAN, CAPTAIN MARVEL JUNIOR'S ALTER EGO.

SOMETIMES THE DAYDREAMING THAT YOU DO WHEN YOU'RE CREATING SENDS YOU IN ODD DIRECTIONS. I WAS THINKING ABOUT THOR HEYERDAHL AND HIS MEMOIR, "KON-TIKI," WHERE HE RIDES A BOAT TO EASTER ISLAND. I GAVE MY THOR EASTER-ISLAND-LOOKING ANTAGONISTS.

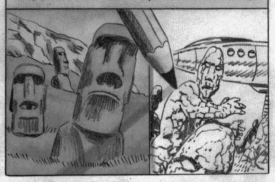

I'M TOO BUSY TO WRITE THE DIALOGUE ON THIS ONE, SO I'M BRINGING IN MY BROTHER LARRY TO DO IT.

I BASED THOR AND LOKI'S RELATIONSHIP TO ODIN ON LARRY AND STAN'S RELATIONSHIP WITH MARTIN GOODMAN. THEY WERE BOTH ALWAYS LOOKING FOR HIS APPROVAL. LARRY WAS GUILELESS AND LOYAL. STAN WAS CONNIVING.

I CREATED IRON MAN. I SET UP THE CONCEPT AND DREW THE COVER BEFORE IT GOT PASSED TO MY FRIEND DON HECK TO DRAW THE COMIC. I DREW A LOT OF COMICS, BUT I COULDN'T DRAW 'EM ALL.

STAN DIDN'T HAVE TIME TO WRITE THE DIALOGUE, SO LARRY WROTE IT. STAN STIFFED ME ON THE PLOT CREDIT. I DON'T KNOW WHICH WAS MORE IMPORTANT TO STAN, THE CREDIT OR THE WRITING FEE.

STAN SAID MARTIN WANTED MORE CONCEPTS. I WAS GOING THROUGH UNUSED SIMON AND KIRBY IDEAS. I DUSTED OFF SPIDERMAN. HE HAD A WEBGUN AND COULD WALK UP WALLS

WHAT HAVE YOU GOT THERE, JACK?

I WAS GOING THROUGH SOME OLD FILES AND I FOUND THIS.

SPIDERMAN?

I WAS TOO BUSY TO WORK ON IT, SO LIKE WITH IRON MAN, WE PASSED IT OFF TO A DIFFERENT ARTIST. STEVE DITKO HAD BEEN DOING GREAT WORK WITH STAN ON THE MONSTER BOOKS SO HE GOT THE SPIDERMAN ASSIGNMENT.

DITKO WAS THE PERFECT CHOICE. HE BROUGHT A WEIRDNESS TO THE CHARACTER THAT WAS PERFECT. HE TOSSED OUT A LOT OF WHAT I DID AND MADE A STRIP THAT MADE SENSE TO HIM. IF I'D HAVE DONE THE STRIP, IT WOULDN'T HAVE BEEN THE BREAKOUT SUCCESS IT WAS.

THE HALLOWEEN COSTUME COMPANY "BEN COOPER" THREATENED MARVEL WITH LEGAL ACTION. THEY HAD A COSTUME CALLED "SPIDER MAN" THAT CAME OUT A DECADE BEFORE THE COMIC.

MARTIN MUST HAVE MADE SOME KIND OF DEAL WITH THEM AFTER THAT BECAUSE PRETTY SOON BEN COOPER WAS PRODUCING THE FIRST LICENSED MARVEL PRODUCTS, HALLOWEEN COSTUMES.

TRICK OR TREAT!

GOOD EVENING, MY FELLOW CITIZENS. THIS GOVERNMENT, AS PROMISED, HAS MAINTAINED THE CLOSEST SURVEILLANCE OF THE SOVIET MILITARY BUILDUP ON THE ISLAND OF CUBA.

THE PURPOSE OF THESE BASES CAN BE NONE OTHER THAN TO PROVIDE NUCLEAR STRIKE CAPABILITY...

I STARTED THINKING ABOUT THE POSTATOMIC FUTURES OF THE PULPS. WHAT IF THAT WORLD CAME TODAY?

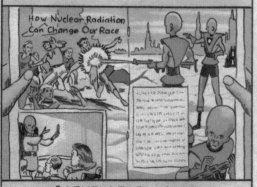

How Nuclear Radiation Can Change Our Race

I REMEMBERED AN OLD "MECHANIX ILLUSTRATED" ARTICLE TALKING ABOUT "MUTANTS" AND "HOMO SUPERIOR."

IT WAS A FURTHER DEVELOPMENT OF THEMES FROM FANTASTIC FOUR, BUT THAT ANY ONE OF US COULD WAKE UP ONE DAY AND REALIZE WE WERE THE MUTANTS.

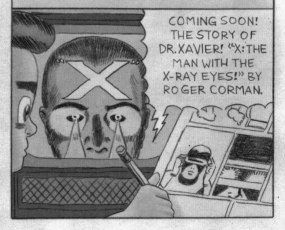

COMING SOON! THE STORY OF DR. XAVIER! "X: THE MAN WITH THE X-RAY EYES!" BY ROGER CORMAN.

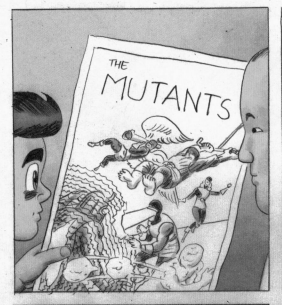

MARTIN SAID WE'RE GOING TO HAVE TO CHANGE THE NAME OF THE BOOK. HE THINKS "THE MUTANTS" IS TOO SCIENTIFIC AND IT'LL GO OVER THE KIDS' HEADS.

IF X-RAYS CAUSE THE MUTATIONS, WE'LL CALL THEM THE X-MEN.

THEY FOUGHT FOR THE FUTURE OF MANKIND. THE BROTHERHOOD OF EVIL MUTANTS WANTED TO SUBJUGATE HUMANITY, THE X-MEN WANTED TO COEXIST IN PEACE. THIS DIFFERENCE IN PHILOSOPHY LED TO A SECRET WAR BETWEEN THE GOOD AND EVIL MUTANTS.

IT WAS A SETUP THAT HAD BIG POTENTIAL. GOOD AND EVIL CHARACTERS COULD LOGICALLY POP UP FROM ANYWHERE. PROFESSOR X USED HIS CEREBRO COMPUTER TO FIND AND RECRUIT THEM BEFORE MAGNETO COULD.

FEAR WAS STOKED BY POLITICIANS, LEADING TO THE CREATION OF GIANT SENTINEL ROBOTS TO SEEK OUT AND DESTROY ALL MUTANTS.

I AM THE JUGGERNAUT! YOUR LONG LOST BROTHER!

EVENTUALLY I STOPPED FULLY DRAWING IT. I'D DO THE COVERS, OF COURSE, BUT I'D DO PLOTS AND LAYOUTS FOR OTHER ARTISTS TO FOLLOW. THEN I STOPPED WORKING ON THE INSIDES ALTOGETHER.

IT WAS A LOT EASIER BEFORE MARVEL COMICS STARTED TAKING OFF. I HAD THE BIGGEST WORKLOAD OF MY LIFE, BUT I HAD TO KEEP GOING. I HAD MORE WORK THAN EVER, BUT MORE MOUTHS TO FEED THAN EVER AND NO PIECE OF THE PROFITS OF MY LABOR. JUST A ONE-TIME PAYMENT.

MUSIC AND LAUGHTER FILLED OUR HOUSE. I MADE SURE TO SPEND TIME WITH THE KIDS DURING THEIR WAKING HOURS. IT WAS A TOUGH BALANCE TO STRIKE.

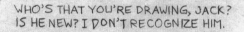

WHO'S THAT YOU'RE DRAWING, JACK? IS HE NEW? I DON'T RECOGNIZE HIM.

IT'S AN OLD COMIC STRIP PITCH I DID A WHILE BACK FOR THE SYNDICATES. IT'S ABOUT A GANG OF MISFITS IN WORLD WAR II. I THINK I'M GONNA BRING IT TO STAN.

SO HE CAN PUT HIS NAME ON IT AND SAY "WRITTEN BY STAN LEE"?

YOU'RE GIVING THEM AN AWFUL LOT OF ORIGINAL STUFF. THAT'S A LOT OF SLEEPLESS NIGHTS. I HOPE THEY APPRECIATE YOU.

ALL THAT MATTERS RIGHT NOW IS THAT THE BOOKS SELL.

IF THE BOOKS SELL, WE EAT. WE KEEP A ROOF OVER OUR HEADS.

MARTIN WANTS TO SEE IF WE CAN DO ANYTHING WITH SOME TRADEMARKS THAT ARE UP FOR GRABS. "DAREDEVIL." "CAPTAIN MARVEL." NAMES THAT MEANT SOMETHING IN THE OLD DAYS.

IT WAS THE SAME FORMULA AS THE HUMAN TORCH AND SUB-MARINER IN THE FANTASTIC FOUR. TAKE A GOLDEN AGE SUPERHERO AND BRING IT INTO THE MODERN AGE.

HMM... FIRST OFF, A CHARACTER CALLED DARE "DEVIL" SHOULD HAVE SOME HORN.

I CAME UP WITH SOME CONCEPTS FOR THE CHARACTER AND DESIGNED HIS COSTUME. I DREW A COVER IMAGE.

THE NEXT ISSUE OF FANTASTIC FOUR IS DUE TOMORROW. I'M GONNA HAVE TO PUT THIS ASIDE FOR NOW.

I DIDN'T HAVE TIME TO KEEP WORKING ON IT. BILL EVERETT TOOK OVER THE ASSIGNMENT.

HIS TRICK CANE TURNS INTO A BILLY CLUB.

BILL WAS ONE OF THE GREATS OF THE INDUSTRY. HIS SUB-MARINER WAS A CORNERSTONE OF THE OLD MARVEL.

BILL'S LATE WITH THAT DAREDEVIL BOOK, SO NOW WE'VE GOT A HOLE IN THE SCHEDULE WE NEED TO FILL. MARTIN'S BEEN ON ME TO DO A "JUSTICE LEAGUE." MAYBE WE LITERALLY DO THAT. TAKE A BUNCH OF OUR HEROES AND PUT THEM ON A TEAM TOGETHER.

WE QUICKLY HASHED OUT A BASIC PLOT. I WENT HOME AND DREW IT.

MARTIN WANTED US TO TEAM UP HUMAN TORCH, SUB-MARINER, AND CAPTAIN AMERICA, BUT WE WENT WITH OUR NEW CHARACTERS. IT FLOWED ORGANICALLY OUT OF OUR ESTABLISHED STORYLINES IN THE CHARACTERS' OTHER BOOKS.

WE NAMED THE GROUP AFTER AN OLD PULP HERO CALLED "THE AVENGER."

HEY JACK, IT'S REALLY EXCITING WORKING WITH YOU. I'VE BEEN A BIG FAN MY WHOLE LIFE. YOUR WORK MEANS THE WORLD TO ME.

THANKS, LARRY. I DON'T KNOW WHAT TO SAY.

STAN'S YOUNGER BROTHER LARRY, A TALENTED ARTIST IN HIS OWN RIGHT, WAS WRITING SCRIPTS TO ACCOMPANY MY EARLY ISSUES OF "THOR," "ANTMAN," AND "IRON MAN."

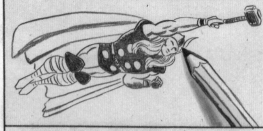

TO ME, IT WAS AFTER-THE-FACT WORK, PUTTING DIALOGUE OVER MY STORIES.

IT WAS THE SAME AS WITH STAN, BUT AT LEAST STAN AND I WOULD SOMETIMES THROW IDEAS BACK AND FORTH BEFORE I STARTED DRAWING. IT WAS HARD WATCHING EVERYBODY BUT ME GET CREDIT FOR MY IDEAS.

WALLY WOOD CAME TO MARVEL LOOKING FOR WORK. STAN WAS EXCITED. HE THOUGHT HE COULD GET A DYNAMIC GOING WITH WALLY LIKE HE HAD WITH ME--HAVING WALLY DO THE HEAVY LIFTING OF THE STORY, THEN WRITE DIALOGUE OVER IT AND TAKE FULL WRITING CREDIT.

HERE HE IS, OUR NEWEST STAR ARTIST!

WALLY HAD HIS OWN REFINED APPROACH. HE RETOOLED DAREDEVIL, STREAMLINING THE LOOK AND STORIES OF THE CHARACTER.

THE HONEYMOON DIDN'T LAST LONG. WALLY DIDN'T LIKE COMING UP WITH STORIES AND NOT GETTING PAY OR CREDIT FOR IT. I DIDN'T LIKE IT EITHER, BUT I HAD A WIFE AND KIDS DEPENDING ON ME. WALLY LEFT MARVEL. STAN TRASHED HIM, HIDING BEHIND JOKES.

WALLY WOOD WROTE **PART ONE** OF THIS TWO-PARTER LAST ISH, JUST FOR A LARK! BUT NOW IT'S UP TO SLY OL' **STAN** TO PUT ALL THE PIECES TOGETHER AND MAKE IT COME OUT OKAY IN THE END! CAN HE **DO** IT? SEE FOR YOURSELF!

I WAS WRITING AND DRAWING ROUGH VERSIONS OF COMICS FOR OTHER ARTISTS TO FINISH. STAN WANTED ME ON AS MANY BOOKS AS POSSIBLE AND THIS WAS THE WAY TO DO IT.

HULK

GEN. ROSS

HULK YELLS YOU CAN'T STOP ME!

I WAS STEERING ALMOST THE WHOLE LINE OF BOOKS, BUT I WASN'T BEING PAID OR CREDITED FOR THE WRITING I DID, WHICH WAS A LOT OF WORK. I WAS PAID A MUCH REDUCED RATE FOR STICK FIGURE DRAWINGS. FIGURING OUT WHAT'S GOING ON IN A COMIC IS A BIG PART OF WRITING A STORY. MY WORK WAS BEING TAKEN FOR GRANTED.

EVEN IF I WASN'T PAID FOR THE WRITING I DID ON MY MAIN BOOKS, AT LEAST I GOT MY FULL ART RATE. ADDING INSULT TO INJURY, STAN CREDITED ME WITH "LAYOUTS," BUT NOT PLOT OR A CO-WRITING CREDIT.

Script: Smilin' STAN LEE
Layouts: Jolly JACK KIRBY
Art: Wild BILL EVERETT
Lettering: Whammy SAMMY ROSEN
Applause: Honest IRVING FORBUSH

I WAS WORKING LONGER HOURS THAN AT ANY POINT IN MY CAREER EXCEPT WHEN I WAS FIRST BREAKING IN. I WAS BURNING THE MIDNIGHT OIL. STAN WANTED TO USE ME ACROSS THE LINE, COORDINATING PLOT THREADS ACROSS MULTIPLE BOOKS. I WAS SPREAD TOO THIN.

IT'S ENOUGH, STAN. I CAN'T DO THESE EXTRA BOOKS FOR JUST THE LAYOUT FEE.

GOSH, JACK. YOU'RE NOT LEAVING ME, ARE YOU?

STAN TOOK ME OFF ALL THOSE "LAYOUT" BOOKS. NOW I WAS DRAWING THOR, FANTASTIC FOUR, CAPTAIN AMERICA, AND THE OCCASIONAL FILL-IN.

WALLY WOOD WENT TO ANOTHER COMPANY, TOWER, AND CREATED HIS OWN SUPERHERO UNIVERSE. HE INVITED ME TO JOIN HIM, BUT I COULDN'T TAKE THE PAY CUT. HE GOT TO TELL HIS OWN STORIES HIS WAY.

STAN AND I HAD OUR DUSTUPS. ONE TIME THINGS GOT BAD. I WALKED OUT OF HIS OFFICE. HE REJECTED A HULK STORY I'D WORKED ON. I WASN'T GOING TO BE PAID FOR MY TROUBLE EITHER. I RIPPED UP THE PAGES AND THREW THEM IN THE GARBAGE.

@ # 𝍇

WHAT ARE YOU DOING, LARRY?

THESE ARE KIRBY PAGES. I'LL TREASURE THESE FOREVER. I'LL STUDY THEM.

WHERE'S THE TAPE, FLO?

I PITCHED A SERIES ENTITLED "THE MAN CALLED D.E.A.T.H." IT WAS A "MAN FROM U.N.C.L.E." RIFF FEATURING NICK FURY, BUT IN THE MODERN DAY. WE ENDED UP SETTLING ON THE TITLE "NICK FURY, AGENT OF S.H.I.E.L.D."

THE MAN CALLED... D.E.A.T.H.!

SGT. FURY WAS NOW A COLONEL AND I GAVE HIM AN EYEPATCH. I ALWAYS IDENTIFIED WITH NICK FURY. HIS WAR STORIES WERE A LARGER-THAN-LIFE VERSION OF MY OWN. I SWEAR TO GOD, AFTER I DREW HIM WITH THAT EYEPATCH, I STARTED LOSING MY VISION IN THE SAME EYE. I SAW SPOTS EVERYWHERE I LOOKED. I DIDN'T REALIZE JUST HOW DEPENDENT I WAS ON HAVING TWO FUNCTIONING EYES.

I NEEDED TO BE MORE CAREFUL WHICH CHARACTERS I IDENTIFY WITH AND WHAT HAPPENS TO THEM.

I WENT TO LUNCH WITH GIL KANE AND A COUPLE OF ARTISTS.

I'LL RIP HIS HEAD OFF! I'LL BREAK HIS ARMS. HE DOESN'T KNOW WHO HE'S DEALING WITH!

WE ALL HAD OUR FRUSTRATIONS IN THE BUSINESS, BUT IT WAS REALLY STARTING TO BUILD UP FOR ME.

I WROTE THE FULL SCRIPT FOR "FANTASTIC FOUR" #6. I FILLED IN THE BALLOONS, AND STAN DIDN'T CHANGE A WORD, BUT SIGNED HIS NAME TO IT.

AN UNSUNG HERO OF THE MARVEL OFFICE WAS SOL BRODSKY, THE OFFICE MANAGER. HE DID IT ALL.

PEOPLE LIKE HIM ARE THE FOUNDATION OF THIS BUSINESS. HE MADE SURE PEOPLE GOT PAID, ARTISTS HIT THEIR DEADLINES, ART GOT TO THE PRINTER, AND HE DID IT WITH A SMILE.

THE MARVEL SUPERHEROES WERE A HUGE SUCCESS AND IT GOT THE INDUSTRY OUT OF A SWAMP.

STAN TOLD THE OTHER ARTISTS TO DRAW LIKE ME. HE HAD A WHOLE SPIEL. SOMETIMES STAN WOULD HAVE ME DRAW A COUPLE OF PAGES TO GET THEM STARTED.

SOON, THE WRITERS AND ARTISTS AT DC STARTED IMITATING ME.

ALL OUR CHARACTERS SEEMED TO EXIST IN THE SAME WORLD. EVENTS FROM ONE BOOK WOULD IMPACT THE OTHERS. WHEN A CHARACTER DIDN'T HAVE A HOME, LIKE ANT-MAN AND WASP AND THE HULK AFTER THEIR BOOKS WERE CANCELLED, THEY COULD STAY IN FRONT OF THE PUBLIC AS GUEST STARS IN OUR OTHER BOOKS.

I WORKED FAST. PLOTS AND CONCEPTS WERE REUSED AND RECYCLED, BUT EACH TIME I GAVE THEM NEW WRINKLES AND ADDED DEPTH. THE MARVEL UNIVERSE WAS TAKING SHAPE A LITTLE BIT AT A TIME.

THE WATCHER WAS A CONCEPT I CRIBBED FROM THE PULPS. IN THE PULP VERSION, THE WATCHERS WERE AN ANCIENT RACE FROM A BLUE PLANET. OUR VERSION LIVED ON THE BLUE AREA OF THE MOON AND WATCHED MANKIND EVOLVE.

THE STORY OUTGREW TYPICAL SUPERVILLAIN CHARACTERS LIKE THE RED GHOST AND HIS SUPER APES. THE WATCHER POINTED THE WAY TO A NEW TYPE OF COMIC STORY, THE COSMIC SUPERHERO.

WHILE HULK NO LONGER HAD HIS OWN BOOK, STAN AND I BELIEVED IN HIM. HE WAS AN UNBEATABLE OPPONENT WHO'D TEST OUR HEROES' METTLE. SOMETIMES HE'D SURPRISE YOU WITH A GOOD DEED. HE WAS A WILD CARD. EVENTUALLY WE FOUND A SPOT FOR HIM IN "TALES TO ASTONISH" WITH SUB-MARINER.

JOHN F. KENNEDY MADE AN APPEARANCE IN FANTASTIC FOUR. I WAS A LIFE LONG ROOSEVELT DEMOCRAT AND KENNEDY WAS AN EXCITING YOUNG PRESIDENT. FOR THE FIRST TIME, THE PRESIDENT WAS YOUNGER THAN ME.

WE MUST SHOW HIM THAT THE UNITED STATES CANNOT BE THREATENED BY ANYONE! WE MUST MOVE FORWARD AND PROCEED WITH GREAT VIGOR! AND NOW, GENTLEMEN, IF YOU'LL EXCUSE ME, IT'S CAROLINE'S BEDTIME!

WE BROUGHT BACK CAPTAIN AMERICA. FIRST, WE TESTED THE WATERS WITH AN APPEARANCE OF A CAP IMPERSONATOR CROOK IN A HUMAN TORCH STORY IN "STRANGE TALES."

IT'S TIME.

WE DECIDED TO BRING BACK THE REAL CAPTAIN AMERICA IN AN ISSUE OF "AVENGERS." I HAD TO COME UP WITH A COMPELLING EXPLANATION FOR WHERE HE'S BEEN ALL THESE YEARS.

I TOLD THE STORY OF HIS FINAL ILL-FATED MISSION IN WWII.

I THOUGHT OF ALL THE GUYS WHO DIDN'T MAKE IT HOME. HIS PARTNER BUCKY WAS KILLED IN ACTION. CAP FELL IN THE WATER AND WAS FROZEN IN A BLOCK OF ICE, LIKE THE MONSTER IN "FRANKENSTEIN MEETS THE WOLF MAN" OR THE SUSPENDED ANIMATION OF "BUCK ROGERS." THE ICE WAS WHAT SAVED MY LIFE AND GOT ME OUT OF THE WAR.

THE ICE-COVERED CAPTAIN AMERICA BECAME AN IDOL WORSHIPPED AT THE SOUTH POLE.

SPITEFUL SUB-MARINER THROWS THE ICE IDOL INTO THE OCEAN.

CAP THAWS OUT AND IS FOUND BY THE AVENGERS.

LIKE ME, CAP WAS A MAN OUT OF TIME. HE RETURNED TO A WORLD THAT HE DIDN'T RECOGNIZE. THE WAR CHANGED HIM. TIME MOVED ON AND HE KEPT RELIVING THE HELL HE LEFT BEHIND.

HE WAS HAUNTED BY THE TRAGEDY OF THE FRIENDS HE LOST.

I FELT MORE AND MORE LIKE AN OLD MAN OUT OF STEP WITH THINGS. TIMES WERE CHANGING FAST. THE POP ART MOVEMENT CAME ALONG. ANDY WARHOL WAS MAKING PAINTINGS OUT OF SOUP CANS AND SOAP BOXES.

STAN, ALWAYS LOOKING FOR AN ANGLE, CHANGED THE NAME OF MARVEL COMICS TO "MARVEL POP ART PRODUCTIONS."

MARVEL PAPERBACKS? I GUESS I'M A LEGITIMATE AUTHOR NOW. WOULD'VE BEEN NICE IF THEY PAID ME FOR IT, THOUGH.

LOOK, JACK.

GREAT! BUBBLE GUM CARDS, TOO? I'M EVERYWHERE THESE DAYS.

DADDY DREW THESE.

I WAS DRAWING THE BOOKS, ONE AFTER THE OTHER, DOING A BOOK A WEEK. THE STORIES STARTED TO MERGE. THE SCI-FI OF "FANTASTIC FOUR" RUBBED OFF ON THOR. THE MAJESTY AND MYTHOLOGICAL THEMES OF THOR RUBBED OFF ON FF, MAKING IT MORE EPIC.

THE PRESIDENT WAS SHOT AND KILLED IN DALLAS.

THE KIDS CRIED. ME AND ROZ CRIED.

THE WORLD WAS DIFFERENT. UNCERTAIN. I CHANNELED THAT INTO MY WORK.

I COULDN'T DO THE SAME OLD STORIES. THEY WERE SUPERHEROES, BUT I PUT MY REAL EMOTIONS AND ANGUISH INTO THEM.

REED'S DYING--

THE THING'S SECOND CLASH WITH THE HULK WAS THE FIRST THING I DREW AFTER THE KENNEDY ASSASSINATION. IT WAS CATACLYSMIC, A TWO-PARTER WITH LIFE-AND-DEATH STAKES.

I WAS REALLY PROUD OF THAT ONE. I WANTED TO DO MORE LIKE IT.

JACK RUBY SHOT LEE HARVEY OSWALD. THAT WAS WHEN THE SIXTIES BECAME "THE SIXTIES." WE WERE IN UNCHARTED TERRITORY.

TEN YEARS LATER I'D DO A COMIC ABOUT THE LAST DAYS OF JACK RUBY.

11:21 A.M.

YOU KILLED MY PRESIDENT, YOU RAT!

JACK! JACK! YOU SON OF A BITCH!

I HOPE DIES... KNOW

I CREATED "THE LADY IN BLACK" BACK AT DC. I CREATED A SIMILAR CHARACTER AT MARVEL CALLED "THE BLACK WIDOW" FOR IRON MAN. I DREW COVERS BEFORE THEY'D DO THE INTERIORS. A LOT OF TIMES THAT MEANT I'D COME UP WITH THE VILLAIN OR STORY IDEA.

COVERS WERE HOW STAN KEPT MY IDEAS IN MORE BOOKS THAN I COULD DRAW MYSELF. I WAS ABLE TO WORK AT A MORE HUMAN PACE AND MY WORK BLOSSOMED. THIS BECAME THE HEIGHT OF MARVEL.

I HAD TIME TO GILD THE LILY. I DON'T ENJOY RUSHING OR CUTTING CORNERS. I TAKE PRIDE AND ENJOYMENT FROM MY WORK. I LIKE TO PUT IN THE DETAILS THAT NOBODY ELSE WOULD. MY STORIES HAVE A CAST OF THOUSANDS.

NO! NO! NO! DON'T SHOOT! DON'T SHOOT!

JACK, IT'S OKAY. IT'S JUST ME.

I'M GONNA GO DOWN TO THE DUNGEON AND GET SOME WORK DONE.

I DIDN'T SLEEP WELL. I KEPT DREAMING ABOUT FRANCE—ABOUT THE WAR. IT WAS EASIER TO JUST STAY UP LATER AND LATER. THERE WAS ALWAYS WORK TO DO.

I GOT INVITED TO SOMETHING CALLED THE NEW YORK COMICON.

WHAT THE HELL'S A COMICON?

I WAS THE KEYNOTE SPEAKER.

THANK YOU. IT'S THE READERS THAT MAKE EVERYTHING POSSIBLE FOR ME.

COME ON IN, JACK. HAVE A SEAT.

WHAT'S THIS ALL ABOUT, MARTIN?

I APPRECIATE HOW HARD YOU'VE BEEN WORKING FOR THE COMPANY. WE'RE LOOKING TO EXPAND THE LINE.

OUR DISTRIBUTOR IS RELAXING THE LIMIT ON NEW BOOKS, SO WE'RE GOING TO BE GROWING THE COMICS DIVISION. THAT MEANS WE'LL NEED NEW BOOKS, NEW CHARACTERS, NEW COMICS. THAT'LL BE A LOT OF WORK WE'LL BE ABLE TO SEND YOUR WAY.

WELL, MARTIN, I'VE BEEN THINKING. THESE BOOKS HAVE BEEN BIG HITS AND I'D LIKE A PIECE OF ANY NEW CHARACTERS I COME UP WITH. A ROYALTY. A PERCENTAGE.

JACK, YOU'LL GET EVERYTHING YOU DESERVE. WE'RE MAKING DEALS FOR TV SHOWS AND IF THAT HAPPENS WITH ANY OF YOUR BOOKS, YOU'LL BE REWARDED.

I CAME UP WITH THE INHUMANS, A SUPERHERO VERSION OF THE MUNSTERS OR THE ADDAMS FAMILY. SUPER WEIRDIES.

THE IDEA WAS WE'D ROLL OUT THESE NEW CHARACTERS IN "FANTASTIC FOUR" OR "THOR" AND IF THE READERS LIKED THEM, THEY'D GET THEIR OWN BOOKS.

THE STORIES CONTINUED BUILDING OFF OF EACH OTHER. A MEGA EPIC RATHER THAN INDIVIDUAL SHORT STORIES. MORE LIKE A NOVEL. I INTRODUCED ANOTHER NEW CHARACTER THAT COULD POSSIBLY CARRY HIS OWN SERIES: HERCULES.

IN ITALY, THEY WERE MAKING A BUNCH OF MOVIES STARRING STEVE REEVES.

I HAD THE WHOLE GREEK PANTHEON TO USE LIKE THE NORSE GODS IN "THOR." HERCULES WAS AN EQUAL TO THOR. I SPOTLIGHTED THEIR DIFFERENCES. HERCULES WAS BOASTFUL AND CAREFREE. A PARTY GUY. THOR WAS SERIOUS AND DUTY BOUND.

THOR'S FATHER, ODIN, TAKES AWAY THOR'S POWER AT A CRITICAL MOMENT. HERCULES GETS THE BETTER OF THOR AND STEALS HIS GIRL.

THOR GOES INTO A DEEP DEPRESSION. HE FIGHTS TO DEFEND ASGARD FROM ODIN'S CORRUPT ADVISOR. THOR ALMOST DIES IN THE PROCESS.

WHEN THOR FINALLY RECOVERS, THE FIRST THING HE DOES IS HELP HERCULES OUT OF A LIFE-OR-DEATH SITUATION. HERCULES WAS TRAPPED IN HADES BECAUSE HE SIGNED A BAD HOLLYWOOD CONTRACT.

HERCULES IS HUMBLED BY THOR'S GENEROSITY. THEY BECOME FRIENDS FOR LIFE.

STAN HIRED A NEW ASSISTANT EDITOR, ROY THOMAS. ROY WAS A COMICS SUPERFAN. HE WAS A NICE KID, A FORMER SCHOOLTEACHER, BUT HE ASKED A MILLION QUESTIONS ABOUT THE OLD DAYS OF COMICS.

WHY'D YOU CHANGE THE SHAPE OF CAP'S SHIELD?

I LAMPOONED HIM IN "NICK FURY," AS THE YOUNG EAGER BEAVER AGENT SITWELL WHO WOULD ASK NICK AND DUM-DUM DUGAN ABOUT THE OLD DAYS.

MARTIN TELLS ME JOE SIMON IS SUING THE COMPANY FOR OWNERSHIP OF CAPTAIN AMERICA. THE COPYRIGHTS ARE UP FOR RENEWAL. WE MIGHT HAVE TO CANCEL THE BOOK.

I WAS WORKING ON A REPLACEMENT FOR CAPTAIN AMERICA, BUT I DON'T KNOW, SOMETIMES I WONDER IF MARTIN KEEPS BILL EVERETT BUSY SO HE WON'T FIGHT FOR OWNERSHIP OF SUB-MARINER. ARE THEY DOING THE SAME THING WITH ME AND CAPTAIN AMERICA?

STAN WENT ON VACATION FOR THE FIRST TIME. HE LET ME PUT THE FINAL WORDS IN THE BALLOONS ON THE ISSUE OF "S.H.I.E.L.D." I WAS WORKING ON. I FINALLY GOT CREDIT FOR WRITING SOMETHING.

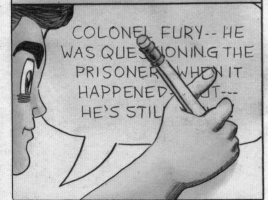

COLONEL FURY-- HE WAS QUESTIONING THE PRISONER WHEN IT HAPPENED, BUT--- HE'S STILL

WE WERE GETTING CLOSE TO ISSUE #50 ON "FANTASTIC FOUR." I THOUGHT WE SHOULD DO SOMETHING SPECIAL FOR IT. WE HAD THE WEDDING OF MR. FANTASTIC AND INVISIBLE GIRL IN THE PREVIOUS ANNUAL. HOW DO YOU TOP THAT? I WENT TO THE BIBLE.

AN ALL-CONSUMING SPACE GOD COMES TO EARTH CALLED GALACTUS. HE'S A WORLD-EATER, SEE? HE COMES TO A PLANET, CONVERTS ALL ITS LIFE, ALL ITS WATER INTO A FORM OF ELEMENTAL ENERGY HE CAN FEED OFF OF. HE LEAVES BEHIND A DEAD HUSK.

I LIKE IT!

I WENT HOME AND STARTED DRAWING. I FIGURED ANY GUY AS HIGH FALUTIN AS GALACTUS WOULD NEED A HERALD TO ANNOUNCE HIS ARRIVAL. A SPACE GOD AND HIS SPACE ANGEL.

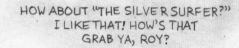

JACK, THESE LOOK GREAT.

BUT WHO'S THIS GUY?

I CALL HIM "THE SURFER."

HOW ABOUT "THE SILVER SURFER?" I LIKE THAT! HOW'S THAT GRAB YA, ROY?

THE SURFER TURNS AGAINST HIS GOD GALACTUS AND IS EXILED ON EARTH-- A FALLEN ANGEL.

I WALKED IN ONE DAY AND STAN LOOKED DIFFERENT. HE HAD FLASHY CLOTHES AND SEEMED TO HAVE GROWN A FULL HEAD OF HAIR OVERNIGHT.

STANLEY?

HEY, JACKIE BABY!

COLLEGES WOULD ASK MARVEL TO SEND ONE OF ITS ARTISTS TO GIVE A TALK AND STAN WOULD SHOW UP AND PUT ON A SONG AND DANCE. THE POPULARITY OF THE COMICS WAS GOING TO HIS HEAD.

IF MY COMICS REFLECTED REALITY, IT COULDN'T BE ALL WHITE FACES. I CAME UP WITH COAL TIGER.

I TINKERED WITH THE CHARACTER AND HE BECAME THE BLACK PANTHER.

STAN HAD THE PRODUCTION DEPT. MAKE SOME LAST-MINUTE CHANGES.

AHH... MY PREY LEARNS QUICKLY! THEY HAVE ELECTED TO STOP AND PLAN BEFORE PLUNGING WIT- LESSLY INTO ANOTHER FOOL- HARDY ATTACK!

THAT IS GOO A VICTORY TO EASILY WON TOO SOON FORGOTTE

BLACK PANTHER MADE HIS DEBUT IN FANTASTIC FOUR #52. HE WAS KING OF THE AFRICAN NATION OF WAKANDA, THE MOST TECHNOLOGICALLY ADVANCED COUNTRY ON THE PLANET.

A SERIES OF CARTOONS BASED ON MY COMICS HIT THE AIR.

THEY TOOK MY DRAWINGS AND FILMED THEM. THEY SHOOK THE CAMERA AND MOVED THE MOUTHS ON MY PICTURES. I GOT NO CREDIT, NO MONEY. THOSE WERE MY DRAWINGS. I'D NEVER SEEN ANYTHING LIKE IT. IT WAS SHAMELESS.

A REPORTER WAS WORKING ON A FEATURE ABOUT STAN AND ME FOR THE "NEW YORK HERALD TRIBUNE." THE REPORTER SAT IN ON ONE OF OUR STORY CONFERENCES.

STANLEY WAS JUMPING ON THE DESK, WAVING HIS ARMS LIKE A CRAZY MAN. I JUST SAT THERE AND WATCHED HIM. IT WAS NUTTY.

WHEN IT WAS OVER, I SAID A FEW WORDS AND WENT BACK TO WORK. THE ARTICLE COMES OUT AND THE GUY WRITES ABOUT WHAT AN AMAZING WRITER STANLEY IS. WHO COULD WORK LIKE THAT? BY THE TIME HE WAS DONE JUMPING AROUND I COULD HAVE THREE PAGES DONE.

WE TOLD OUR FRIENDS AND FAMILY TO LOOK OUT FOR THE ARTICLE.

"HIGH-PITCHED"?! "YEAH YEAH"?! THE WAY THEY WRITE ABOUT ME MAKES ME SOUND LIKE A JERK--LIKE A YES MAN.

I DON'T LIKE THIS ARTICLE. IT MAKES IT SOUND LIKE YOU DO EVERYTHING AND I DO NOTHING. THE CREDITS IN OUR BOOKS DON'T SAY ANY DIFFERENT.

THE BOOKS SAY "WRITTEN BY STAN LEE." THESE ARE STORIES I BRING TO YOU. SOMETIMES WE HASH OUT A STORY TOGETHER, BUT A LOT OF THE TIME THESE ARE MY IDEAS, MY STORIES. SURE, YOU PUT DIALOGUE IN, BUT THAT'S AFTER I'VE TOLD THE STORY. AFTER ALL THAT, IT STILL SAYS "WRITTEN BY STAN LEE."

I'M GETTING NO CREDIT FOR THE WRITING I'M DOING JUST BECAUSE YOU'RE FILLING THE BALLOONS. AS FAR AS THE WORLD'S CONCERNED, I'M JUST THE GUY WHO ILLUSTRATES YOUR GENIUS.

I'VE HAD ENOUGH, STANLEY!

OKAY, JACK. OKAY. I CAN SEE THIS IS SOMETHING YOU'RE VERY PASSIONATE ABOUT. I'LL SEE WHAT I CAN DO.

SO STANLEY CHANGED THE CREDITS TO SAY...

A STAN LEE - JACK KIRBY PRODUCTION
INKED BY: VINCE COLLETTA
LETTERED BY: SAM ROSEN
(MAY THEIR ARMOR NEVER TARNISH!)

I DON'T KNOW WHY "WRITTEN BY STAN LEE AND JACK KIRBY" WOULDN'T WORK. I COULD GUESS AT STAN'S MOTIVES, BUT THIS WAS AN IMPROVEMENT.

THE SUPERHERO COMEBACK WAS IN FULL SWING. THE OLD SUPERMAN SHOW WAS STILL IN RERUNS, BUT A NEW COLORFUL POP ART BATMAN TV SHOW WAS A BIG HIT.

THE LEGAL BATTLE FOR OWNERSHIP OF THE COPYRIGHT FOR CAPTAIN AMERICA CONTINUED BETWEEN JOE SIMON AND MARTIN GOODMAN. IF I WANTED TO CLAIM A PIECE IT WOULD MEAN SUING MY CURRENT BOSS.

Last Will and Testament...

SIGN THIS, JACK.

WHAT IS IT?

IT'S A DEPOSITION AGAINST JOE'S LEGAL CLAIM TO CAPTAIN AMERICA. YOU'D BE SAYING YOU CREATED CAPTAIN AMERICA AT OUR DIRECTION, NOT SOMETHING YOU CAME UP WITH ON YOUR OWN.

WHAT COULD I DO? IT WAS LIKE THE SKY MASTERS/JACK SCHIFF SITUATION ALL OVER AGAIN. MARVEL WAS MY BREAD AND BUTTER. IF I DIDN'T PLAY BALL, I COULD BE ON MY ASS AGAIN.

WE'LL PAY YOU A GENEROUS BUYOUT.

WHAT ABOUT JOE?

WE'RE OFFERING HIM THE SAME DEAL. YOU'LL BOTH GET THE SAME AMOUNT. 50/50.

I DON'T KNOW, MARTIN. THIS IS A LOT TO THINK ABOUT.

YEARS LATER I FOUND OUT THEY'D LIED TO ME. JOE GOT A BIG OUT-OF-COURT SETTLEMENT WHILE I SIGNED AWAY MY RIGHTS FOR PENNIES ON THE DOLLAR.

A NEW GENERATION OF YOUNG ARTISTS WERE COMING IN TO HANDLE THE EXPANSION OF THE LINE. THESE KIDS WERE FANS OF WHAT WE'D DONE.

THERE WAS BARRY SMITH, FROM ENGLAND. HE TRIED REALLY HARD TO DRAW LIKE ME AT FIRST. HE EVENTUALLY DEVELOPED HIS OWN AWARD-WINNING STYLE. I ENCOURAGED EVERY ARTIST WHO ASKED ME FOR ADVICE TO DO THINGS THEIR OWN WAY.

HERB TRIMPE WAS A QUIET GUY. HE DREW HIS COMICS IN THE OFFICE AND WAS AVAILABLE FOR LITTLE TASKS HERE AND THERE. HE WAS A VIETNAM VET. HE SPENT A LOT OF TIME AT THE DRAWING BOARD. HE TRIED TO DRAW LIKE ME, TOO.

NEAL ADAMS WAS THE MOST TALENTED ARTIST AT DC. IT WAS A COUP WHEN STAN BROUGHT HIM OVER TO DO "X-MEN" FOR US.

JIM STERANKO WAS A SMARTLY DRESSED YOUNG DYNAMO. HE HAD A UNIQUE APPROACH. HIS FIRST JOB AT MARVEL WAS DOING THE FINISHES ON MY LAYOUTS FOR "NICK FURY." I COULD SEE MY INFLUENCE, BUT HE TOOK IT IN NEW INNOVATIVE DIRECTIONS.

THAT PAGE IS TOO BEAUTIFUL TO GIVE MARVEL. YOU SHOULD KEEP THAT ONE.

DON'T WASTE IT ON THEM. THEY DON'T DESERVE IT.

A "FANTASTIC FOUR" CARTOON CAME OUT. IT WAS PRETTY GOOD. OF COURSE IT WAS! THEY WERE USING MY STORIES. I CREATED A SENSATION AND HAD NO REAL CONNECTION TO IT.

I CREATED THESE THINGS IN MY HOUSE. THEY MADE MILLIONS FOR SOMEBODY-- NOT ME. AT LEAST MY NAME WAS ON IT.

SOME KIDS FROM THE UNIVERSITY OF SOUTHERN CALIFORNIA ASKED IF I WOULD DESIGN SOME COSTUMES FOR THEIR PRODUCTION OF "JULIUS CAESAR." THE CHALLENGE INTRIGUED ME. I KNEW I COULD DO SOMETHING UNIQUE WITH THAT.

THIS IS GREAT!

MY DESIGNS--ALIVE AND IN COLOR! WHAT A THRILL.

STEVE DITKO WAS QUIET AND RESERVED, BUT HE CONFIDED IN ME ABOUT HIS GROWING FRUSTRATIONS.

I WRITE THESE STORIES, JACK. I GIVE THEM TO STAN AND HE TURNS THEM ON THEIR HEAD--INVERTS THEIR MEANING. MEANING AND CLARITY DON'T MEAN ANYTHING TO STAN, BUT THE MESSAGE IS THE MOST IMPORTANT THING TO ME.

I KNOW, STEVE. I'M HAVING THE SAME PROBLEMS WITH STANLEY. I LIKE THE FREEDOM, BUT I WANT CREDIT FOR MY WORK. I WANT TO BE PAID FOR THE WRITING I DO, BUT WHENEVER I BRING IT UP TO STAN, HE DEFLECTS OR GETS HISTRIONIC IF I REALLY PUSH THE ISSUE.

STEVE DITKO HAD ENOUGH. HE LEFT MARVEL, LEFT SPIDER-MAN, LEFT DR. STRANGE.

YOU SHOULD COME WITH ME, JACK. YOU'RE NEVER GOING TO GET FAIR AND EQUITABLE TREATMENT FROM STAN.

WHAT WAS I GOING TO DO? MY NAME WAS MUD AT DC AS LONG AS SCHIFF WAS THERE. I WASN'T ABOUT TO GO WORK FOR CONNECTICUT.

I WISH YOU ALL THE LUCK IN THE WORLD, STEVE, BUT I GOTTA STAY HERE AND FIGHT THE GOOD FIGHT.

HE WENT ACROSS THE STREET TO DC COMICS. HE DID WORK FOR WALLY WOOD'S TOWER COMICS AND FOR CHARLTON, THE CONNECTICUT OUTFIT. HE DID ORIGINALS FOR FANZINES.

NOTHING HE DID SUCCEEDED LIKE SPIDER-MAN, BUT PERSONAL INTEGRITY WAS THE MOST IMPORTANT THING TO STEVE. HE WASN'T WILLING TO SACRIFICE THAT FOR POPULARITY.

I HAD A BUNCH OF CONCEPTS TO START A NEW LINE OF BOOKS, A NEW UNIVERSE. THE MARVEL STORIES WERE GETTING STALE. WE NEEDED TO INTRODUCE THE NEXT THING.

I DID CONCEPT DRAWINGS FOR THE VARIOUS CHARACTERS. THE STACK KEPT GROWING, BUT SOMETHING IN MY GUT WAS KEEPING ME FROM BRINGING THESE ONES TO STANLEY.

I DID SOME COLLAGE FOR THE REALLY IMPORTANT CHARACTERS.

WE SHOULD KILL EVERYBODY OFF IN THOR. THE NORSE RAGNAROK, THEN START FROM SCRATCH WITH A NEW PANTHEON OF NEW GODS. MODERN GODS FOR A MODERN AGE.

THOR IS ONE OF OUR BIGGEST SELLERS. WHY MESS WITH PERFECTION?

THOSE IDEAS WERE TOO GOOD FOR THEM ANYWAY.

ROZ AND I HAD DINNER WITH JIM STERANKO. HE REGALED US WITH TALES OF HIS ESCAPE ARTIST CAREER.

"ESCAPE ARTIST"? I PREFER THE TERM "LIBERATIONIST."

I LEARNED MY TRADE FROM MY MISSPENT YOUTH AND FROM MY FATHER'S BAG OF MAGIC TRICKS FROM HIS SHORT-LIVED CAREER AS A STAGE MAGICIAN. I WAS A CRIMINAL, A JUVENILE DELINQUENT. I INVENTED WAYS OF GETTING INTO AND OUT OF JAMS. WHERE MOST LIBERATIONISTS GO WRONG IS THEY DON'T STAY AHEAD OF TECHNOLOGY. I INVENTED A NUMBER OF DEVICES TO AID MY ESCAPES. I DEVISED MY OWN ADHESIVE I REFERRED TO AS GRAVITY GLUE. IT ALLOWED ME TO...

I CAME UP WITH THE SUPER ESCAPE ARTIST, MISTER MIRACLE, A YOUNG APPRENTICE FOLLOWING IN THE FOOTSTEPS OF AN OLD MASTER. HE STAYED ONE STEP AHEAD OF THE DICKENSIAN CHARACTERS FROM HIS MISSPENT YOUTH ON A PRISON PLANET.

YOU'RE DOING A SILVER SURFER COMIC WITHOUT ME?

WELL, JACK, YOU'RE SO BUSY SO I JUST THOUGHT...

THE SURFER IS MY BABY.

THE SILVER SURFER IS MY BABY, TOO. TRUST ME, JACKSON. I'LL TAKE GOOD CARE OF HIM.

AT THE 1968 PHIL SEULING COMIC ART CONVENTION, I WAS GIVEN AN ALLEY AWARD FOR BEST PENCILLER. A BUNCH OF STORIES I DID THAT YEAR WON ALLEY AWARDS, TOO.

THANK YOU. THIS MEANS THE WORLD TO ME.

STEVE DITKO WASN'T EASY TO REPLACE. HE CO-WROTE, PENCILLED, AND INKED DR. STRANGE AND SPIDER-MAN. STANLEY NEEDED A WHOLE ROOM WITH THREE PEOPLE--MARIE SEVERIN, JOHN ROMITA, AND ROY THOMAS--TO DO WHAT STEVE DITKO DID ALL BY HIMSELF.

STEVE DITKO WAS AN ADHERENT TO AYN RAND'S OBJECTIVIST PHILOSOPHY. I WROTE A STORY ABOUT THE DANGERS OF THAT WORLDVIEW. I CREATED A CHARACTER WHO GREW OUT OF A COCOON. I CALLED HIM COCOON MAN. STAN CHANGED THE CHARACTER'S NAME TO "HIM." IT WAS A STORY ABOUT WELL-INTENTIONED SCIENTISTS CREATING A SUPERBEING.

STAN CHANGED THE STORY SO THAT THEY WERE STANDARD-ISSUE CACKLING MAD SCIENTISTS. THE POINT I WAS TRYING TO MAKE WAS LOST. I WAS GETTING FED UP. I WAS COMING UP WITH STORIES AND STAN WAS UNDERMINING THEM WITH ARBITRARY CHANGES SEEMINGLY JUST TO JUSTIFY HIS CREDIT. HE WROTE IN DIALOGUE THAT SABOTAGED THE WHOLE POINT OF THE STORIES.

MARTIN WAS SELLING THE COMPANY TO A BIG CONGLOMERATE, PERFECT FILM & CHEMICALS. THOSE ROYALTIES HE PROMISED ME STILL WEREN'T COMING. IF I DIDN'T NAIL DOWN OUR HANDSHAKE AGREEMENTS BEFORE THE DEAL WENT THROUGH, THOSE PROMISES WOULD BE COMPLETELY WORTHLESS.

PERFECT FILM & CHEMICAL CORP

STAN DID HIS SILVER SURFER SERIES WITHOUT ME, ONE OF THE CHARACTERS I CREATED AFTER MARTIN'S PROMISED "CUT" OF THE PROFITS. STAN'S NEW ORIGIN COMPLETELY CONTRADICTED WHAT MADE THE CHARACTER WORK.

I'M THROWING MY HANDS IN THE AIR. I'M NOT GONNA GIVE THEM ANOTHER SILVER SURFER.

I'M NOT CREATING ANYTHING NEW FOR THEM.

I COULDN'T HELP MYSELF. I GET BORED DOING THE SAME OLD THING. I KEPT COMING UP WITH NEW CONCEPTS AND CHARACTERS IN THE BOOKS, BUT THE BEST ONES I SAVED FOR MYSELF.

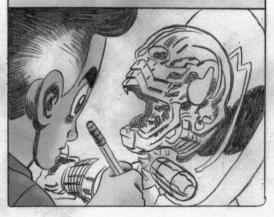

MARTIN, I NEED YOU TO MAKE GOOD ON THOSE PROMISES YOU MADE ABOUT A PIECE OF THE ACTION FROM THE NEW CHARACTERS.

SORRY, JACK. THIS IS THE BEST I CAN DO FOR YOU RIGHT NOW. YOU'RE MAKING MORE MONEY THAN ANY ARTIST IN THE INDUSTRY.

WHAT'VE YOU GOT FOR ME THERE, JACKSON? A NEW VILLAIN FOR THE NEXT ISSUE OF FANTASTIC FOUR? LEMME SEE!

NO, IT'S NOTHING. JUST SOME BLANK PAPER.

BUT I DO HAVE AN IDEA I'VE BEEN THINKING ABOUT FOR A WHILE.

I HAD MY STACK OF NEW GODS THAT WE COULD'VE INTRODUCED THROUGH THOR'S TALES OF ASGARD BACKUP, BUT...

I THINK WE SHOULD END TALES OF ASGARD. ALL THAT MYTHOLOGY JAZZ HAS RUN ITS COURSE

I HAD TO FIGHT MY IMPULSE TO SHOW STANLEY MY NEW GODS. I'D HAVE NOBODY TO BLAME BUT MYSELF IF I HANDED OVER ANOTHER SILVER SURFER.

IF STANLEY WANTED NEW CHARACTERS, HE COULD COME UP WITH THEM HIMSELF. IF I'M JUST THE ILLUSTRATOR, THEN I'LL JUST ILLUSTRATE.

LET ME TELL YOU, THE IDEAS HE BROUGHT ME WERE REAL STINKERS -- LIKE "THE MAN CALLED MONOCLE."

MY DAUGHTER HAD ASTHMA, SO WE DECIDED TO MOVE OUT TO CALIFORNIA FOR THE FRESH AIR.

MARTIN LENT ME $2,000 AGAINST FUTURE EARNINGS TO PAY FOR THE MOVE.

I HATE TO SEE YOU GO, JACKSON.

BE CAREFUL WITH THAT DESK, IT'S HOW I MAKE MY LIVING.

THE NEW HOUSE WAS BIG AND EMPTY AND FULL OF POSSIBILITY. THE KIDS WERE EXCITED ABOUT THE SWIMMING POOL.

WE HAD QUIET. WE HAD FRESH CALIFORNIA AIR.

THE HELL?!

ROAAAAR

MOTORCYCLE GANGS USED THE VALLEY BELOW MY HOUSE AS A DRAG STRIP.

SHEL DORF CAME TO MY HOUSE. HE RAN A COMICS CLUB AND WAS STARTING A CONVENTION IN SAN DIEGO. HE BROUGHT SOME YOUNG COMICS FANS WITH HIM TO MEET ME.

JACK SCHIFF RETIRED AT DC, FOLLOWED BY MORT WEISINGER, WHO HATED ME AND MY WORK. NOW THE IDEA OF JUMPING SHIP TO DC WASN'T AN IMPOSSIBILITY.

I GOT TO MEET SUPERMAN CREATORS SIEGEL AND SHUSTER. I THANKED THEM PROFUSELY FOR GIVING ME A CAREER.

I'D BEEN IN TOUCH WITH DC PUBLISHER CARMINE INFANTINO. HE LET ME KNOW THE DOOR WAS OPEN AT DC. I INVITED HIM TO THE PASSOVER SEDER AT MY HOUSE.

I SHOWED MY NEW CONCEPTS TO HIM-- THE ONES I DIDN'T SHOW STANLEY.

I TOLD HIM, "WHEN THE OLD GODS DIED, THERE AROSE THE NEW GODS."

I TOLD HIM MY PLAN FOR THE NEXT PHASE OF THOR... A STORY ABOUT A NEW PANTHEON OF GODS.

I'D KILL OFF ALL OF THE GODS IN RAGNAROK, A FIERY LAST BATTLE, THEN LAUNCH A LINE OF NEW BOOKS, THE ADVENTURES OF A NEW RACE OF GODS BASED NOT ON THE CIVILIZATION OF THE VIKINGS, BUT BASED ON TODAY.

I LOVE IT, JACK.

A COMPANY CALLED MARVELMANIA WAS THE OFFICIAL MARVEL FAN CLUB. THEY PUBLISHED A MAGAZINE AND A SERIES OF POSTERS. I WAS IMPRESSED WITH THE WRITING OF TWO OF THE KIDS ON STAFF, STEVE SHERMAN AND MARK EVANIER. THE GUY STEERING THE SHIP WAS A DIFFERENT STORY.

MARVELMANIA PROMISED A LOT AND DELIVERED LITTLE. HE TOOK DRAWINGS I DID, AND GOT OTHER ARTISTS TO TINKER WITH 'EM AND TOOK MY NAME OFF.

JACK KIRBY

HERB TRIMPE

IT WAS A FLY-BY-NIGHT OUTFIT. A LOT OF KIDS SENT IN THEIR SHEKELS AND NEVER GOT THEIR POSTERS. I FELT BAD FOR STEVE AND MARK, TOO, WHO WERE OUT OF A JOB AND OWED BACK PAY.

I FLEW TO NEW YORK TO FINALIZE NEGOTIATIONS ON MY NEW CONTRACT WITH MARVEL.

THINGS DIDN'T GET BETTER, THEY GOT WORSE.

TAKE IT OR LEAVE IT.

I DIDN'T SIGN IT. NOW I WAS WORKING WITHOUT A CONTRACT.

THEN I GOT THE CALL FROM MY BROTHER, DAVE.

JACK...MOM DIED.

MY MOTHER WAS EVERYTHING. IN MY NEIGHBORHOOD, MOTHERS WERE REVERED. SHE'S THE ONE WHO TAUGHT ME HOW TO TELL STORIES. I WENT TO HER FOR ADVICE. SHE WAS WARM. SHE WAS NO-NONSENSE. SHE WOULDN'T LET ME FEEL SORRY FOR MYSELF.

THE WORK DOESN'T STOP.

THE DEATH TOLL IN VIETNAM REACHES A NEW HIGH...

FOUR KENT STATE STUDENTS SHOT AND KILLED BY NATIONAL GUARDSMEN...

I CREATED CAPTAIN AMERICA.

STAN LEE CREATED CAPTAIN AMERICA.

EVER SINCE MARTIN SOLD MARVEL, THE NEW OWNERS DIDN'T KNOW ME FROM ADAM. I WAS GONNA GET LESS FROM MARVEL, NOT MORE. NONE OF THE THINGS I WAS PROMISED WERE GOING TO BE DELIVERED. THAT WAS REALITY.

YOU COULD ALWAYS LEAVE.

IN A MOMENT OF SENTIMENTALITY I WROTE A HORROR STORY WITH TWO MYSTERIOUS HOODED FIGURES TELLING THE STORY OF A MISUNDERSTOOD QUASIMODO CHARACTER WHO CREATED ROBOTS TO KEEP HIM COMPANY.

THE HOODED FIGURES TELLING THE STORY REMOVE THEIR HOODS REVEALING ME AND STAN.

MYSTERY IS RESOLVED-- SHALL WE UNMASK NOW?

OUR TALE IS TOLD--

WHEN STAN GOT THROUGH WITH IT, THE STORY WAS GUTTED. THE SYMPATHETIC HUNCHBACK BECAME ANOTHER CACKLING VILLAIN. HE HAD ANOTHER ARTIST REDRAW THE MONSTER. WORST OF ALL, STAN REMOVED OUR CAMEO FROM THE STORY.

STAN KEPT ME OFF THE SERIES, BUT I DID THE FINAL ISSUE OF "SILVER SURFER." I PUT ALL OF MY FRUSTRATIONS INTO IT.

I'M GOING TO MAKE YOU PAY!

I CAME IN ONE NIGHT AND THERE WAS STAN LEE TALKING INTO A RECORDER, SITTING IN THE DARK. IT WAS STRANGE TO ME. I FELT THAT WE WERE GOING IN DIFFERENT DIRECTIONS. I REALIZED I WAS CREATING SOMETHING I DIDN'T WANT TO CREATE. THERE'S A NOVEL, "WHAT MAKES SAMMY RUN" BY BUDD SCHULBERG. SAMMY, IN THAT BOOK, IS THE KIND OF A CHARACTER YOU WOULDN'T WANT TO BE RESPONSIBLE FOR DEVELOPING. I FELT THAT I WAS DEVELOPING A SAMMY-- WHICH I WAS, IN STAN LEE. I FELT IT WAS MY TIME TO GO.

I SENT IN MY LAST "FANTASTIC FOUR" ISSUE. I CALLED STAN AND TOLD HIM THE NEWS.

I QUIT.

MARIE SEVERIN PINNED UP A TRIBUTE TO MY DEPARTURE ON THE BULLETIN BOARD IN THE MARVEL BULLPEN.

143

DC AND CARMINE WERE MY TICKET OUT, BUT WE HIT A SNAG.

JACK, I LOVE YOUR NEW CONCEPTS, AND I LOVE YOU. HERE'S THE PROBLEM. I MENTIONED IT TO THE EDITORS AND THEY SAID, "WE DON'T LIKE MARVEL AND WE DON'T LIKE JACK." I'VE GOT A MUTINY ON MY HANDS.

I SPOKE TO CARMINE'S BOSS. MY OLD FRIEND JACK LIEBOWITZ.

KIRBY, SUPERMAN NEEDS A SHOT IN THE ARM. HE'S GROWN STALE. HE'S A PRODUCT OF THE THIRTIES. I WANT A SUPERMAN FOR THE SEVENTIES. I WANT YOU TO TAKE OVER SUPERMAN. GIVE HIM WHAT YOU GAVE YOUR MARVEL BOOKS.

SUPERMAN, SEE, HE'S AN ALIEN IN A WORLD OF INFERIORS. EVERYBODY'S AFRAID OF HIM. EVERYBODY'S INTIMIDATED BY HIM, LOTS OF RESENTMENT. IN MY NEIGHBORHOOD, THE TOUGHEST GUY ON THE BLOCK HAD A TARGET ON HIS BACK. EVERYBODY WANTED TO MAKE THEIR REPUTATION BY TAKING HIM DOWN. THAT'S SUPERMAN. THE FINEST MINDS ARE TRYING TO TAKE HIM DOWN. AND WITH THE WAY TECHNOLOGY'S GOING, THEY'RE GONNA COME UP WITH SOMETHING SOONER OR LATER.

FIRST THING YOU GOTTA DO IS GET RID OF KRYPTONITE. IT'S OLD. IT'S BORING. YOU GOTTA COME UP WITH CHARACTERS THAT ARE TOUGHER THAN SUPERMAN. STRONGER, MEANER. MY NEW GODS ARE A MATCH FOR SUPERMAN. DARKSEID COULD CUT SUPERMAN IN HALF. SUPERMAN'S ON THE DEFENSIVE NOW, AND HE DOESN'T HAVE TO HOLD BACK, EITHER.

AND AMONG THE GODS, SUPERMAN FINDS A PLACE WHERE HE MIGHT BELONG. A NEW HOME, MAYBE. PEOPLE HE CAN RELATE TO. PEOPLE WHO KNOW WHAT IT'S LIKE TO FLY WITH THE EAGLES.

BUT PARADISE IS DENIED FOR SUPERMAN. AS LONG AS EARTH IS THREATENED BY DARKSEID'S SUPER WAR, SUPERMAN HAS TO FOREGO HIS OWN HAPPINESS AND STAY WHERE HE'S NEEDED... WHERE THE ACTION IS.

SOUNDS GOOD, JACK.

I MADE MY FIRST NEW COMIC FOR THEM. I INTRODUCED AS MUCH OF THIS STUFF AS I COULD.

WAIT! THIS IS MY ONLY CHANCE TO FIND MY OWN KIND! YOU MUST TELL ME HOW TO REACH SUPER TOWN!

NOW I WAS FILLING IN THE BALLOONS. I DID EVERYTHING I DID WHEN I WORKED FOR STANLEY, BUT SOMEHOW I WASN'T CALLED A WRITER SINCE I DIDN'T FILL IN THE BALLOONS.

WITH SUPERMAN IN THE PICTURE, THE FIGHT GAME IS A FARCE!

IF ONLY I COULD MEET HIM ON HIS OWN TERMS--!

YES--I-I SEE YOUR VIEWPOINT, ROCKY--

I INTRODUCED THE VILLAIN THAT WOULD LINK ALL THE BOOKS, DARKSEID, THE GOD OF EVIL.

I RELEASE HER TO YOUR CUSTODY--

THERE ARE OTHERS WHO CAN SOLVE THE EQUATION!

ONE OF THEM SHALL YIELD TO ME!

WE TRANSMIT GRAVITY WAVES FROM HEAVY MASS GALAXIES-- WE CAN HOLD ANY SUPER-BEING!

IT'S TRUE-- THERE IS INCREDIBLE, CRUSHING WEIGHT BEING CHANNELED INTO MY BODY!

PARADISE IS WITHIN SUPERMAN'S GRASP, BUT HE MUST DENY HIMSELF. HIS DUTY IS TO THE PEOPLE OF EARTH AS LONG AS DARKSEID IS ABROAD.

AND AS THE BOOM TUBE FADES, SUPERMAN CATCHES A GLIMPSE OF DISTANT, GLEAMING TOWERS...

THEN, LIKE A DREAM, TOO FADE AND ARE

IT WAS THE WRONG TIME TO GO--

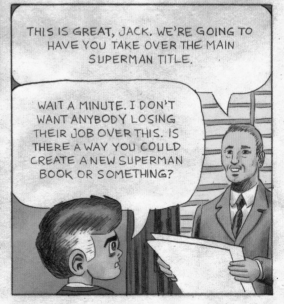

THIS IS GREAT, JACK. WE'RE GOING TO HAVE YOU TAKE OVER THE MAIN SUPERMAN TITLE.

WAIT A MINUTE. I DON'T WANT ANYBODY LOSING THEIR JOB OVER THIS. IS THERE A WAY YOU COULD CREATE A NEW SUPERMAN BOOK OR SOMETHING?

YOU KNOW WHAT, "JIMMY OLSEN" DOESN'T HAVE A REGULAR CREATIVE TEAM. WHY DON'T YOU TAKE OVER THAT BOOK. I'LL WARN YOU, THE BOOK ISN'T DOING SO HOT. IT'S BEEN SLOWLY GOING DOWN THE TOILET SINCE THE SUPERMAN TV SHOW GOT CANCELED.

I'LL DO IT. I CAN MAKE ANYTHING A HIT.

I DID THE FIRST ISSUE OF "JIMMY OLSEN." I BROUGHT IN MORE OF MY CONCEPTS. NEW THINGS-- THE THINGS I WAS HOLDING BACK WHEN I WORKED AT MARVEL.

the word from high is-- THE GREAT ONE IS COMING!

THEY RAN BIG ADS IN THEIR BOOKS TRUMPETING MY ARRIVAL. FINALLY I WAS AT A PLACE WHERE I WAS APPRECIATED.

I WANT YOU TO INTRODUCE THE NEW GODS IN "SHOWCASE COMICS," LIKE YOU DID WITH "CHALLENGERS OF THE UNKNOWN." IT LETS EVERYBODY KNOW IT'S SPECIAL.

IT WOULD DO THE OPPOSITE--MAKES IT SEEM LIKE YOU DON'T BELIEVE IN IT. IT NEEDS ITS OWN BOOK. A "NUMBER ONE" TO MAKE A BIG SPLASH.

SO THIS WAS MY DEAL AT NATIONAL-- CREATE IDEAS FOR NEW BOOKS AND NEW LINES OF BOOKS. I WANTED TO HAVE BETTER PRODUCTION. FULL COLOR GLOSSY MAGAZINES WITH GROWN-UP STORIES. I HIRED STEVE AND MARK, THE KIDS FROM MARVELMANIA, TO BE MY ASSISTANTS.

JOE AND I CAME UP WITH THE ROMANCE COMIC BACK IN THE FORTIES. NOW I CAME UP WITH THE ANTI-ROMANCE COMIC FOR THE SEVENTIES: TRUE DIVORCE STORIES. I PITCHED A DRACULA ANTHOLOGY MAGAZINE, STORIES OF DRACULA THROUGHOUT THE AGES.

I WAS GOING TO EDIT A LINE OF BOOKS. I'D BE HEADING UP DC WEST COAST. FOR NOW I WAS RUNNING IT OUT OF MY HOUSE.

STEVE AND MARK WERE GOING TO WRITE FOR ME AND HANDLE PRODUCTION TASKS. THEY WROTE TEXT PIECES AND HANDLED THE LETTER COLUMNS FOR THE COMICS. THEY HAD A LOT OF ENTHUSIASM, BUT FOR NOW CARMINE WANTED ME TO WRITE AND DRAW ALL THE BOOKS MYSELF. ONCE THE BOOKS WERE ESTABLISHED, THEN I COULD START DELEGATING.

I WAS FASCINATED WITH ITALIAN FUMETTI PHOTO COMICS. WE DID A PROPOSAL CALLED "TEENAGENT," STARRING MY SON NEAL. I TOOK PICTURES OF HIM DOING SPY STUFF. I COLLAGED IT INTO A PHOTO COMIC.

I CALLED UP JOHN ROMITA.

I'M DOING A LINE OF BOOKS FOR NATIONAL. I WANT YOU TO WORK ON ONE OF THEM. IT'S CALLED "MISTER MIRACLE." HOW WOULD YOU LIKE TO DRAW IT?

JOHN REPLACED DITKO ON SPIDER-MAN. HE HAD A CLEAN POLISHED STYLE, WITH ATTRACTIVE HEROES AND HEROINES.

HE CUT HIS TEETH ON CAPTAIN AMERICA, BUT REALLY FLOURISHED ON THE ROMANCE BOOKS IN THE FIFTIES. HE COMBINED THOSE APPROACHES INTO SOMETHING REALLY GREAT.

SORRY, JACK. I'D LOVE TO, BUT I'M HAPPY WITH MARVEL AND STAN.

I CALLED STEVE DITKO.

HE WAS INTRIGUED, BUT BY THIS POINT HE WAS DOING HIS OWN CONCEPTS FOR DC.

"THE FOREVER PEOPLE" WERE TEENAGERS FROM THE PLANET NEW GENESIS, HOME OF THE NEW GODS. THE FOREVER PEOPLE WERE YOUNG PACIFISTS LIVING IN A TIME OF WAR.

FOREVER PEOPLE

THEY SAY THEIR MAGIC WORD AND MERGE TO FORM INFINITY MAN,

ORION STARRED IN THE MAIN BOOK, "NEW GODS." HE GOES TO THE HELL WORLD OF APOKOLIPS TO CONFRONT THE EVIL DARKSEID. HE FOLLOWS HIM TO EARTH, WHERE THE WAR WILL BE WON OR LOST.

WHAT ORION DOESN'T KNOW IS THAT THE EVIL DARKSEID IS HIS FATHER,

ONE OF THE THINGS THAT LINKED MY NEW BOOKS WERE THE TECHNOLOGIES LIKE THE TELEPORTATION DEVICE -- THE BOOM TUBE -- AND THE LIVING, LOVING COMPUTER -- THE MOTHER BOX.

SCOTT FREE IS "MISTER MIRACLE," THE SUPER ESCAPE ARTIST THAT WAS INSPIRED BY JIM STERANKO.

HE'S ESCAPED LIFE IN AN APOKOLIPS ORPHANAGE AND WANTS NOTHING TO DO WITH THE GODS AND THEIR WAR. HE WANTS ONLY TO LIVE IN PEACE AND DEVELOP HIS ART, BUT HE CAN'T ESCAPE HIS PAST.

CARMINE WASN'T READY FOR ME TO HAND OFF THE BOOKS TO OTHER ARTISTS JUST YET, LET ALONE OTHER WRITERS. IN THE MEANTIME STEVE AND MARK WERE PITCHING IDEAS FOR NEW MAGAZINES.

IT LOOKS GREAT!

SUPERWORLD OF EVERYTHING

YOU'RE DOING SUCH A GREAT JOB, JUST KEEP WORKING ON THE BOOKS YOURSELF FOR A LITTLE LONGER.

BIG BARDA WAS A NEW ADDITION TO THE MISTER MIRACLE CAST. A FRIEND FROM HIS PAST TO BALANCE OUT ALL HIS CHILDHOOD ENEMIES. SHE STOOD OUT IN AN ALREADY COLORFUL CAST.

YES, THIS IS A FAR CRY FROM OUR DAYS AS PUPILS OF GRANNY GOODNESS!

THERE'S LOTS TO TALK ABOUT, BARDA THAT IS-- IF I WALK OUT OF THIS BUILDING IN ONE PIECE!

THERE WAS A LIMIT TO HOW MANY BOOKS I COULD DO MYSELF, SO I HAD HIGH HOPES FOR A BIG BARDA SPIN-OFF IDEA. HOPEFULLY THIS COULD BE THE BOOK I COULD OVERSEE WITHOUT DRAWING.

BIG BARDA AND THE FEMALE FURIES

I WANTED TO CREATE ANOTHER MARVEL WITHIN D.C. I PUT MY FULL EFFORT INTO THESE BOOKS. AS A RESULT, I WAS DOING THE BEST WORK OF MY CAREER. THESE STORIES MEANT A LOT TO ME PERSONALLY.

IT'S AN INTERLOCKING UNIVERSE OF CHARACTERS, BUT CREATED SMARTLY, NOT ARBITRARILY-- CREATED WITH A PLAN. A NOVEL IN COMIC BOOK FORM. WHAT I'VE DONE IS COME IN WITH THE WHOLE BALL OF WAX, PLOPPED IT DOWN, AND I'M GOING TO ASK EVERYONE'S PATIENCE TO ALLOW ME TO UNRAVEL IT.

WE DID OUR OWN "UNDERGROUND" COMIC--"UNCLE CARMINE'S FAT CITY COMIX." I GOT DITKO, WALLY WOOD, AND THE WRITER HARLAN ELLISON TO CONTRIBUTE A PAGE EACH. I DID MY FIRST AND ONLY FORAY INTO "ADULT" THEMED COMICS, "GALAXY GREEN."

ASTRO-CHICKS

CARMINE NIXED THE IDEA ALONG WITH "SOUL LOVE" AND "TRUE DIVORCE." THE COLOR MAGAZINES I'D PITCHED GOT SCALED DOWN TO BLACK-AND-WHITE MAGS, TO TRY TO EMULATE THE SUCCESS AND LOW PRODUCTION COSTS OF "MAD" AND THE WARREN MAGAZINES LIKE "CREEPY."

"JIMMY OLSEN" WAS THE FIRST OF MY NEW COMICS TO HIT THE STANDS. SALES WERE HUGE, A BIG BUMP UP FROM THE PREVIOUS ISSUES.

JUST WAIT 'TIL MY ORIGINAL BOOKS HIT THE SHELVES!

I GOT A RUDE SHOCK WHEN MY COPIES OF "JIMMY OLSEN" ARRIVED.

WHAT THE--!?

I NEVER DREW THAT.

SOMEBODY IN THE NEW YORK OFFICE REDREW ALL OF MY SUPERMAN AND JIMMY OLSEN FIGURES.

CARMINE, WHAT'S THE DEAL?

THE SUPERMAN OFFICE FELT LIKE YOUR SUPERMAN LOOKED TOO DIFFERENT.

ISN'T THAT WHY YOU HIRED ME? TO DO A NEW KIND OF SUPERMAN?

SUPERMAN IS BIGGER THAN JUST THE COMICS. HE'S ON LUNCH BOXES, TOYS, AND WHISTLES. WE NEED TO KEEP A CONSISTENT IMAGE TO PROTECT THE TRADEMARK.

VINNIE COLLETTA WAS INKING FOR MARVEL AND DC. HE WAS BRINGING AROUND MY TOP SECRET NEW PAGES TO MARVEL AND THEY WERE MAKING COPIES AND PASSING THEM AROUND THE OFFICE.

I DID A CHARACTER CALLED "COUNT DRAGORIN," A SCI-FI VAMPIRE FOR AN UPCOMING ISSUE OF "JIMMY OLSEN." I SWEAR THEY COPIED COUNT DRAGORIN FROM THE PAGES VINNIE SHOWED THEM WHEN THEY MADE "MORBIUS THE LIVING VAMPIRE" AT MARVEL. THEY RUSHED THE CHARACTER INTO PRODUCTION AND MADE MINE LOOK LIKE THE RIP-OFF.

DRAGORIN

MORBIUS

WHEN I FOUND OUT COLLETTA WAS SHOWING MY WORK AROUND THE OFFICE OF THE COMPETITION, I WAS FURIOUS.

MARK AND STEVE HAD BEEN SHOWING ME INSTANCES WHERE VINNIE WAS DELETING CHARACTERS FROM MY DRAWINGS TO MAKE HIS JOB EASIER. IT WAS THE LAST STRAW. I DON'T USUALLY GET TOO INVOLVED WITH INKERS, BUT I GAVE VINNIE A CALL.

YEAH, I SHOWED YOUR STUFF TO MARVEL. SO WHAT?

I COULD LOOK PAST ALL THE CORNERS YOU CUT, BUT SHOWING MY WORK TO THE COMPETITION IS INEXCUSABLE.

CUTTING CORNERS? I'M THE FASTEST INKER IN THE BUSINESS. THAT'S WHAT THEY PAY ME FOR.

THERE'S NO TWO WAYS ABOUT IT. YOU'RE FIRED, VINNIE!

GOOD LUCK, KIRBY. YOU'RE DONE. YOUR BEST YEARS ARE BEHIND YOU. YOUR BOOKS ARE DUDS AND NOBODY WANTS TO TELL YOU. WITHOUT STAN YOU'RE NOTHING.

I TOLD CARMINE THAT VINNIE WAS OUT.

I INSISTED ON MIKE ROYER. I DIDN'T WANT ANOTHER INKER WHO WAS GOING TO TAKE MY WORK TO MARVEL SO THEY COULD STEAL FROM ME.

OKAY, JACK, BUT THE OFFICE ISN'T GONNA LIKE IT. VINNIE IS VERY POPULAR HERE.

I CAME UP WITH A CHARACTER CALLED THE BLACK RACER WHO I WAS GOING TO USE IN AN ANTHOLOGY SERIES, BUT I GOT NERVOUS MARVEL MIGHT STEAL THE IDEA, SO I PUT HIM IN "NEW GODS."

FOOLISH ONE! WAS IT NOT TOLD TO YOU ON NEW GENESIS OF THE BLACK RACER'S SUPERB AGILITY?

YOU CANNOT ESCAPE ME!

HE WAS A PARAPLEGIC VIETNAM VET WHO BECOMES THE GOD OF DEATH ON SKIS.

I GOT WORD MY BROTHER DAVID DIED OF A HEART ATTACK--MY BABY BROTHER.

DAVID LOVED BOATS, LOVED THE WATER, I DID A LITTLE TRIBUTE TO HIM IN THE CHARACTER OF THE AQUATIC NEW GOD SEAGRIN.

A GENTLE WARRIOR!

ORION GIVES SEAGRIN THE NEW GODS VERSION OF A VIKING FUNERAL. THE BLACK RACER CARRIES HIM BACK TO MYSTICAL SOURCE OF ALL THINGS.

BAROOM

LOOK OUT! THE WHOLE PIER IS GOING UP!

VIKARASSHH

RIDE THE TEMPEST, SEAGRIN! ENTER THE COSMIC FIRE! THE SOURCE WILL TAKE YOU AS A WARRIOR WHO HAS GIVEN ALL!

MIKE ROYER BROUGHT IN HIS FIRST FINISHED INKING ASSIGNMENT.

WHAT THE HELL'S THIS?!

WHAT'S WITH THE FACES?!

I DON'T KNOW. I PRETTIED HER UP, MADE HER LOOK MORE LIKE CHER. DIDN'T JOE SINNOTT EMBELLISH?

I DON'T NEED ANYBODY PRETTYING UP MY PICTURES-- ESPECIALLY THE FACES. I HIRED YOU BECAUSE YOU STICK TO WHAT I LAY DOWN. I DON'T WANT YOU CHANGING A GODDAMN LINE! YOU UNDERSTAND?

MY SON NEAL GOT A JOB WORKING FOR XEROX AND BROUGHT ME HOME AN EARLY PHOTOCOPIER. I STILL HAD THE XEROXES OF MY PENCILS SO I HAD MARK AND STEVE CUT ROYER'S FACES OUT AND PASTED MY FACES IN FROM THE PENCIL PHOTOCOPIES.

I THINK MY BLOWUP PUT THE FEAR OF GOD INTO ROYER BECAUSE FROM THAT POINT FORWARD, HE DIDN'T CHANGE A LINE. HE WAS THE MOST FAITHFUL INKER I EVER HAD... AND MY PERSONAL FAVORITE.

CARMINE WANTED THE "PLANET OF THE APES" LICENSE, BUT LOST IT TO MARVEL. HE ASKED ME TO DO A COMIC IN A SIMILAR VEIN. I OFFERED UP "KAMANDI, LAST BOY ON EARTH," BASED ON MY OLD CONCEPT "KAMANDI OF THE CAVES."

MARK EVANIER CAN WRITE KAMANDI AND DAN SPIEGLE CAN DRAW IT.

YOU'RE NOT GOING TO DRAW IT? YOU'RE NOT GOING TO WRITE IT? THEN WE'RE NOT INTERESTED.

WHAT HAPPENED TO DC COMICS WEST? EVERY TIME I COME UP WITH A BOOK THAT I OVERSEE, YOU INSIST I DRAW IT.

I FINISHED THE FIRST ISSUE OF KAMANDI. I GAVE IT MY ALL.

I GOT MORE AND MORE VISITS AT THE HOUSE. IT WAS A UFO CULT ON THEIR WAY TO MEET THE MOTHER SHIP. WE INVITED THEM IN AND ROZ MADE SANDWICHES FOR EVERYBODY.

CARMINE SHOWED ME A NEAL ADAMS COVER HE WAS PARTICULARLY PROUD OF. CARMINE SAID IT WAS THE HEIGHT OF COMIC ART.

I DON'T LIKE IT. THERE ARE ALL THESE ACTION HEROES AND THEY'RE ALL JUST STANDING AROUND GRINNING WITH THEIR HANDS ON THEIR HIPS. THEY SHOULD BE LEAPING AND TUMBLING AND COLLIDING. THIS IS WHAT'S WRONG WITH DC'S APPROACH.

IN MY OFF HOURS I WAS WRITING A NOVEL, "THE HORDE." IT WAS BASED ON A RECURRING NIGHTMARE I HAD ABOUT A GATHERING MASS OF HUMANITY LED BY A CHARISMATIC LEADER THAT TOOK OVER THE WORLD.

STAN WAS WORKING ON HIS BOOK.

"THE ORIGINS OF MARVEL COMICS."

VARIETY ANNOUNCED AN UPCOMING "SILVER SURFER" MOVIE STARRING DENNIS WILSON OF THE BEACH BOYS.

MARVEL'S SILVER SURFER

JOE SINNOTT INKED "THE FANTASTIC FOUR" ALL THROUGH THE SIXTIES, ALMOST EVERY ISSUE I WORKED ON. WE WERE A WINNING COMBO, BUT I DIDN'T MEET HIM IN PERSON UNTIL AFTER OUR COLLABORATION HAD FINISHED. WE MET FOR THE FIRST TIME AT SAN DIEGO COMICCON.

THE GLOSSY MAGAZINES AND NEW FORMATS NEVER CAME ABOUT. I WAS DOING COMICS IN THE SAME OLD TIRED FORMAT. IF "NEW GODS" AND THE OTHER BOOKS WERE MY JOB, I PUT ALL MY YEARS OF EXPERIENCE INTO THEM.

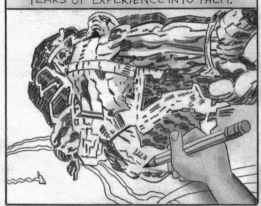

EACH ISSUE WAS A NEW PERSONAL BEST, A COMPLETELY ORIGINAL MYTHOLOGY, A STORY OF LOSS AND REDEMPTION.

I WAS TOLD I'D FIND MY FATHER HERE! IF YOU'RE MY FATHER...SPEAK!

YOU WON'T SPEAK TO ME! YOU'LL NEVER SPEAK TO ME! YOU HATE ME!! HATE ME!!

"HATE" IS NO LONGER A WORD IN THIS PLACE! PUT DOWN THAT WEAPON!! --SON--!

YOU!-- YOU ARE -- MY FATHER??

ONLY IF YOU WISH ME TO BE! I AM HIGHFATHER!

AND YOU--ARE ORION! WE HAVE NEED OF EACH OTHER, ORION! THIS IS A PLACE OF FRIENDS!! HERE IS MY HAND--!!

NO! I--I--

THEY WERE EXTRAPOLATIONS OF THINGS I'D LIVED THROUGH. WARS--THE RISE OF FASCISM--BULLIES BIG AND SMALL.

THIS IS NO TIME FOR JOKES, FRIEND! CAN'T YOU SEE THIS CHILD IS FRIGHTENED?!

OF COURSE, FRIEND. ALL YOUNG HUMANS RECOGNIZE THE REAL THING WHEN THEY SEE IT.

YOUNG HUMANS SEE ME-- EVEN IN "HAPPYLAND" BUT YOU ELDERS HIDE ME WITH "COCK AND BULL" STORIES TO KEEP THE PREMISES SMELLING SWEET!!

FOOL!

AND STILL, THE COSMIC JOKE ESCAPES HIM FOR HOW CAN HE COPE WITH ME-- BY SHUNNING ME--HIS OTHER FACE.

DARKSEID'S MASSIVE FEATURES CRACK WIDE WITH THE LAUGHTER OF APOKOLIPS! BUT THE SOUND OF IT IS DROWNED BY THE MELODIOUS MUSIC OF "HAPPYLAND"

APOKOLIPS AND ITS ARMAGETTO WERE EXTREME VERSIONS OF MY CHILDHOOD IN THE GHETTO AND THE STRANGE PERSONALITIES THAT EMERGED THERE.

STAND CLEAR OF THAT AERO-CARRIER!! PREPARE TO RECEIVE ITS CARGO!!!

NO CODDLING!! NO FALTERING!! NO WHINING!! RUN THEM ALL THE WAY TO THE BARRACKS!!!

THERE WAS DEEP DESPAIR, BUT ALSO GREAT HOPE. EVERYONE HAD THEIR STORY. IT WAS A TAPESTRY IN COMICS FORM ACROSS FOUR DIFFERENT SERIES--A TETRALOGY. THE FOURTH WORLD. I WON A SHAZAM AWARD FOR IT.

HE CAN TAKE IT! I'LL NOT STOP HIM NOW! IF COURAGE AND BRAVERY TOOK HIM HERE!--- SOME OF IT WAS MINE!

STAY, WARRIOR! LET ME COMPLETE THE DESTRUCTION OF SCOTT FREE-- SO YOU MAY LIVE WITH THE MAJESTY THAT IS THE POWER OF DARKSEID!

STAN LEE'S "ORIGINS OF MARVEL COMICS" WAS RELEASED. HE TOLD THE STORY OF THE CREATION OF THE MARVEL CHARACTERS.

I BOUGHT A COPY. I READ PAGE AFTER PAGE OF STAN TAKING SOLE CREDIT AS "CREATOR," WHILE I WAS MERELY "CHOSEN" TO DRAW HIS IDEAS.

IT'S ALL LIES.

I CUT OUT SOME OF THE MORE OFFENSIVE PASSAGES IN THE BOOK.

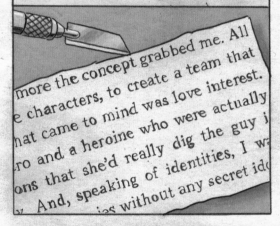

more the concept grabbed me. All
e characters, to create a team that
hat came to mind was love interest.
ero and a heroine who were actually
ons that she'd really dig the guy j
And, speaking of identities, I w
without any secret id

I CAME UP WITH A CHARACTER IN "MISTER MIRACLE"--FUNKY FLASHMAN-- A BIG-TALKING PROMOTER WHO TAKES ALL THE CREDIT AND THE CASH FOR MISTER MIRACLE'S ACCOMPLISHMENTS,

HE LIVED IN A DECREPIT OLD HOUSE (OF IDEAS) LIVING OFF AN INHERITANCE FROM A RICH UNCLE, ACCOMPANIED BY HIS VALET HOUSEROY, WHO I BASED ON ROY THOMAS.

I WAS GETTING OUT ALL MY FRUSTRATIONS ABOUT STAN AND MARVEL. SCOTT FREE MIGHT'VE FALLEN FOR HIS SCHTICK, BUT BIG BARDA, MODELLED ON MY ROZ, KNEW HIS TYPE FROM GROWING UP ON APOKOLIPS.

MARVEL NEVER STOPPED REPRINTING MY OLD STORIES. I WAS SOMETIMES CREDITED, BUT NEVER PAID FOR THE REPRINTS. MY NEW BOOKS WERE COMPETING WITH MY OLD ONES.

I WAS BEING CROWDED OUT OF THE MARKET WITH MY OWN WORK, DONE WHEN I WAS TEN YEARS YOUNGER.

I WAS SICK OF WORKING ON "JIMMY OLSEN." IT WAS THE ONE BOOK I DIDN'T EDIT. IT FELL UNDER THE UMBRELLA OF THE SUPERMAN OFFICE, SO THEY KEPT INTERFERING. THEY'D CHANGE MY SUPERMAN FACES. THEY'D NIX STORIES THAT DIDN'T MESH WITH THE OTHER SUPERMAN BOOKS. THEY FINALLY LET MIKE INK IT AND HE FOUND A WAY TO INK MY SUPERMAN FIGURES SO IT FIT THEIR TRADEMARK, BUT STILL LOOKED LIKE MY ART.

IT WAS ENOUGH, THOUGH. I DON'T LIKE HAVING MY PLANS HAMPERED BY COORDINATING WITH OTHER CREATORS. I QUIT "OLSEN" AND IT FREED ME UP FOR OTHER CONCEPTS--MY OWN ORIGINAL CONCEPTS.

METROPOLIS IS JUST WAITING TO TURN ON A GUY WHO NEEDS A BATH!

ME, TOO!

ME, TOO!

WE'RE COMING HOME!

THE END

"OLSEN" WAS CANCELLED A FEW ISSUES AFTER I LEFT.

THE COMICS CODE HAD RELAXED SOME OF ITS RULES, MAKING HORROR COMICS POSSIBLE AGAIN. THEY HAD A HIT WITH "SWAMP THING" AND CARMINE THOUGHT THAT MAYBE HORROR WOULD SAVE THE INDUSTRY. HE WANTED A SUPERHERO/HORROR HYBRID BOOK FROM ME.

HORROR WAS NEVER MY FORTÉ. I WRACKED MY BRAIN TO COME UP WITH AN ANGLE. I DID WHAT I DID WHENEVER I NEEDED A BREAK.

LET'S GO OUT FOR BURGERS AND CHOCOLATE CAKE.

CARMINE THINKS I'M AN IDEA MACHINE. NOBODY'S DOING ANYTHING ORIGINAL IN COMICS, BUT I'M EXPECTED TO JUST KEEP TURNING OUT NEW CONCEPTS.

EVERYBODY IN COMICS IS RIPPING OFF SOMETHING ELSE. YOU'RE THE ONE GUY WHO'S EXPECTED TO BE CONSTANTLY AND CONSISTENTLY ORIGINAL.

THAT'S IT! THAT'S WHAT I'M GONNA DO...AND I KNOW JUST THE THING TO RIP OFF.

AS SOON AS I GOT HOME I FOUND A REPRINT VOLUME OF OLD HAL FOSTER "PRINCE VALIANT" STRIPS.

HAL FOSTER WAS ONE OF MY FAVORITES. I BASED MY APPROACH TO "TALES OF ASGARD" ON HIS TALES OF KNIGHTS AND CHIVALRY.

PRINCE VALIANT DISGUISED HIMSELF AS A DEMON TO FOOL A CASTLEFUL OF BRIGANDS.

AND INTO THE OGRE'S ROOM FLIES A DEMON RIDING A STAFF!

I CREATED MY DEMON BASED ON HIS. I PLACED THE ORIGIN IN THE DAYS OF ARTHUR. IT WAS MERLIN'S DEMON AND IT TOOK ON THE FORM OF MAN AFTER THE FALL OF CAMELOT.

CARMINE LOVED IT. I GOT A PHONE CALL FROM HIM.

WE LOVE THE NEW BOOKS. "DEMON" AND "KAMANDI" ARE JUST SENSATIONAL.

ONE THING, JACK... WE'RE CANCELLING "NEW GODS" AND "FOREVER PEOPLE." THE STORYLINES ARE TOO COMPLEX. THE COLLEGE KIDS REALLY FLAKED OUT OVER IT, BUT THE YOUNGER KIDS JUST CAN'T FOLLOW IT. WE'LL KEEP "MISTER MIRACLE" RUNNING, BUT YOU GOTTA SIMPLIFY IT. NO MORE GOD STUFF.

ARE YOU OKAY, JACK?

THEY KILLED IT. I'M GIVING THEM THE BEST I'VE GOT AND THEY KILLED IT.

I DIDN'T KNOW WHAT TO DO.

CARMINE WANTED SIMPLE. I GAVE HIM SIMPLE. HAUNTED HOUSES, SLAPSTICK. WHODUNNITS. NO MORE GODS, MYTHOLOGY, INTERWOVEN PLOTLINES. NO APOKOLIPS. NO NEW GENESIS. WITH THREE YEARS LEFT ON MY CONTRACT I WAS JUST RUNNING OUT THE CLOCK.

DON'T BEAT ABOUT THE BUSH! YOU WANT TO KNOW WHAT HAPPENED TO THE DESERTER WE RECAPTURED IN THE WOODS!

--HE WAS TAKEN BACK HERE--TO BE PUNISHED BY ME!--MADAME EVIL EYES!

HE NOW SEES THE ERRORS OF HIS WAYS--JUST AS YOU SHALL-- MISTER MEDDLER!

LOOK OUT! HER EYES, THEY--

SPONNG!

IT JUST ACCELERATED THINGS. "MISTER MIRACLE" GOT CANCELLED. WHEN I DID THE FINAL ISSUE, I TRIED TO TIE UP MY GOD EPIC THE BEST I COULD IN TWENTY PAGES.

WHEN SCOTT AND BARDA FEEL THE STAFF'S TOUCH, THEIR UNION IS MADE--

THUS, IT IS DONE!

LOOK!

I CREATED "OMAC: ONE MAN ARMY CORPS." A FRIENDLESS LONER IN A BLEAK DYSTOPIA GETS SUPERPOWERS. IT WAS AN UPDATE OF CAPTAIN AMERICA AND CAPTAIN MARVEL.

I'M OMAC! EVACUATE THIS SECTION! I'M GOING TO DESTROY IT!

I TRIED TO ENVISION THE WORLD OF TOMORROW. DECADES BEFORE VIRTUAL REALITY TECHNOLOGY, "OMAC" HAD MOVIES FED DIRECTLY INTO THE BRAIN.

I HOPE OMAC IS ENJOYING HIS MOVIE.

CHAPTER ONE

EDITED-WRITTEN-DRAWN BY JACK KIRBY

THE NEXT TIME MIKE ROYER DROPPED OFF HIS PAGES, HE HAD NEWS FOR ME.

JACK, I WAS MOUNTAIN CLIMBING AND I HAD A REALIZATION. THERE'S MORE TO LIFE THAN COMICS. I'M QUITTING, BUT I FOUND SOMEBODY TO TAKE OVER FOR ME.

D. BRUCE BERRY ASSISTED MIKE UNTIL HE WAS UP TO SPEED, THEN HE TOOK OVER THE INKING ON ALL MY BOOKS.

WITH SO MANY OF MY BOOKS CANCELLED, THEY NEEDED TO FIND WORK FOR ME TO DO TO FULFILL MY QUOTA. I GOT ASSIGNED TO OTHER PEOPLE'S BOOKS. BOB KANIGHER NEVER LIKED ME OR MY WORK. THEY ASKED ME TO TAKE OVER HIS BOOK "THE LOSERS." I HATED THE NAME. DC'S CULTURE WAS SO NEGATIVE. "THE LOSERS." "INFERIOR FIVE." "DEADMAN."

I TOOK OVER THE BOOK AND STARTED TELLING MY STORIES, MY EXPERIENCES, THE THINGS THAT I SAW IN THE WAR.

UNLIKE "SGT. FURY" IT WASN'T SUPERHEROES IN WAR, IT WAS REAL PEOPLE. I DIDN'T PULL ANY PUNCHES.

I MET WITH MARVEL EDITOR-IN-CHIEF ROY THOMAS AT THE 1974 SAN DIEGO COMIC-CON.

ROY, I'D LIKE TO COME BACK TO MARVEL.

I'LL BE HONEST WITH YOU, JACK.

YOU SAID SOME UNKIND THINGS ABOUT ME.

WHAT? WHEN?

"HOUSEROY."

OH. THAT.

IT'S NOT A BIG DEAL. I DON'T MIND IT SO MUCH, BUT STAN IS STILL HURT ABOUT "FUNKY FLASHMAN." HE FELT IT WAS MEAN-SPIRITED.

CARMINE GOT IT IN HIS HEAD THAT SINCE COMICS SELL REALLY WELL FOR THE FIRST ISSUE, HE'D CREATE A SERIES THAT WAS ALL FIRST ISSUES, CALLED "FIRST ISSUE SPECIAL."

I THINK THAT'S WHY HE CANCELLED SO MANY BOOKS, SO HE COULD MAKE ROOM FOR MORE FIRST ISSUES.

I HAD A CONAN-STYLED HERO CALLED "ATLAS" THAT PREMIERED IN THE DEBUT ISSUE.

THEN I DID A KID GANG FOR THE SEVENTIES CALLED "THE DINGBATS OF DANGER STREET."

I HAD TWO ASSISTANTS, BUT NOTHING FOR THEM TO DO. MARK QUIT. I STILL NEEDED TO FIND WORK TO KEEP STEVE BUSY. HE WROTE UP FILM TREATMENTS BASED ON A COUPLE OF IDEAS I HAD-- "CAPTAIN VICTORY" AND "SILVER STAR."

THE BUZZING HAS SUBSIDED.

WE ALSO CO-WROTE A COMIC CALLED "KOBRA." IT WAS A MODERN VERSION OF "THE CORSICAN BROTHERS" WITH A PSYCHIC CONNECTION BETWEEN TWO SIBLINGS.

I'M NOT GONNA RENEW MY CONTRACT, CARMINE.

GOOD LUCK, JACK. NO HARD FEELINGS.

I'VE GONE AS FAR AS I CAN GO IN THIS BUSINESS. I'M ALMOST 60. COMICS IS WHAT I KNOW. I'M TOO OLD TO START OVER IN SOME OTHER FIELD.

ROY THOMAS TALKED STANLEY INTO HIRING ME. IT DIDN'T TAKE MUCH CONVINCING

I THOUGHT JACK NEVER SHOULD HAVE LEFT IN THE FIRST PLACE. MARVEL IS WHERE HE BELONGS.

WE HAVE A SPECIAL SURPRISE FOR YOU FOLKS. JACK KIRBY IS COMING BACK TO MARVEL. COME ON UP AND JOIN US, JACK.

I WILL ELECTROCUTE YOU IN THE MIND!

"ELECTRIFY," JACK, "ELECTRIFY!"

I HAVE AN IDEA FOR A ROMEO AND JULIET STORY, SEE. TWO ROBOTS FALL IN LOVE, COMMUNICATING OVER RADIO WAVES, SEE. THEN THEY MEET, BUT THEY INSTANTLY VAPORIZE BECAUSE THEY'RE MADE OUT OF OPPOSITE PARTICLES.

I STARTED ON "CAPTAIN AMERICA," MY TRIUMPHANT RETURN TO THE CHARACTER I CO-CREATED. I DID "THE MADBOMB SAGA," A STORY ABOUT BOMBS THAT DROVE PEOPLE CRAZY, SET TO GO OFF ON THE BICENTENNIAL.

THE TEST ISN'T OVER YET!

SAN DIEGO COMIC-CON 1975: I WAS DRAWING FOR AN AUDIENCE. THE THING I'D DO IN MY SPARE ROOM I WAS DOING IN FRONT OF A PACKED HOUSE.

THEN COMES THE DETAIL WORK.

THE MARVEL FAN CLUB MAGAZINE "FOOM" PROCLAIMED MY RETURN TO THE COMPANY.

THE COVER ART WAS DRAWN IN A PASTICHE OF MY STYLE BY JOHN BYRNE AND JOE SINNOTT.

THE MUSEUM OF CARTOON ART OF GREENWICH, CONNECTICUT, HAD AN EXHIBITION OF MY WORK, "KIRBY: A COLLECTION OF THE ARTISTRY OF JACK KIRBY."

JACK, EVERYBODY WOULD LOVE IT IF YOU CAME BACK TO "THE FANTASTIC FOUR." YOU CAN DO ANY STORY YOU WANT, ANY WAY YOU WANT. TOTAL FREEDOM. WE'D JUST NEED SOMEBODY TO DO THE DIALOGUE.

I CAN'T DO THAT. I CAN'T GO BACKWARDS.

I AGREED TO DRAW COVERS FOR "THE FANTASTIC FOUR," THOUGH. I DID A BUNCH OF THEM.

IN MY NEW "CAPTAIN AMERICA" STORY, CAP UNCOVERS A PLOT BY A SECRET SOCIETY THAT WANTS TO UNDO THE AMERICAN REVOLUTION AND BRING BACK RULE BY THE ARISTOCRACY, ALL LEADING UP TO A TERRORIST ATTACK DURING THE BICENTENNIAL.

WE MUST BEWARE OF THE FREEDOM FREAKS!

OH, HE ISN'T REAL, HE'S JUST A COMPOSITE FACE, PUT TOGETHER BY A COMPUTER.

WRITERS WANTED TO WORK WITH ME, BUT I WAS THERE WITH THE UNDERSTANDING THAT I'D WRITE MY OWN STUFF.

JACK, I'D LOVE TO TEAM UP WITH YOU. I GREW UP READING THE BOOKS YOU DID WITH STAN. I'D LIKE TO BE YOUR NEW STAN LEE.

I PUSHED FOR NEW FORMATS. I WANTED TO DO A BIG GLOSSY ADAPTATION OF "2001: A SPACE ODYSSEY."

STANLEY WROTE A SEQUEL TO "ORIGINS OF MARVEL COMICS." I GOT A COPY OUT OF MORBID CURIOSITY. I BRACED MYSELF.

SON OF ORIGINS OF MARVEL COMICS

I WAS SHOCKED HE GAVE ME CREDIT FOR CREATING THE SILVER SURFER.

DC WAS IMPLODING. CARMINE STEPPED DOWN AS PUBLISHER. JEANETTE KAHN TOOK OVER. ONE OF THE FIRST THINGS SHE DID WAS LOOK AT THE BOOKS AND DECIDE THAT "NEW GODS" NEVER SHOULD'VE BEEN CANCELLED. SHE BROUGHT BACK "NEW GODS," BUT AT THIS POINT I WAS UNDER CONTRACT.

JACK, WE ALWAYS THOUGHT "NEW GODS" SHOULD'VE BEEN A MARVEL BOOK. DC WOULDN'T KNOW A GOOD COMIC IF IT BIT 'EM ON THE ASS.

I'VE GOT ANOTHER IDEA THAT'S EVEN BETTER, "RETURN OF THE GODS." IT'S LIKE A SEQUEL TO "CHARIOTS OF THE GODS." "WHAT IF THE ALIEN GODS CAME BACK?"

WE WENT WITH THE TITLE, "THE ETERNALS." THIS TIME I WASN'T GOING TO DO A SLOW BUILDUP LIKE "NEW GODS" ACROSS MULTIPLE TITLES. EACH ISSUE WAS GONNA BE JAM-PACKED WITH REVELATION AND CATACLYSM.

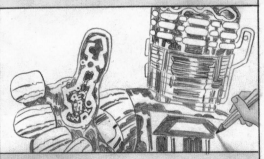

THE GODS WOULD GIVE A THUMBS UP OR A THUMBS DOWN FOR HUMANITY.

MARVEL APPROVED MY "2001: A SPACE ODYSSEY" PITCH, NOT WITH THE GLOSSY MAGAZINE FORMAT I HAD SUGGESTED, BUT AN OVERSIZED TREASURY EDITION. THE FILM MADE A BIG IMPRESSION ON ME. IT CAPTURED THE COSMIC AWE OF THE SCI-FI STORIES I LOVED. IT WAS THE FIRST TIME I COLORED A COMIC SINCE THE FIFTIES.

I WAS STARTING TO FEEL MY AGE. JUST STAYING IN THE CHAIR WAS GETTING TO BE PAINFUL.

VISITING THE MARVEL OFFICES, THERE WERE A LOT OF NEW FACES. I FELT OUT OF PLACE, EVEN THOUGH MY ART AND CHARACTERS WERE PLASTERED ALL OVER THE PLACE.

MARVEL KEPT TEASING "KIRBY'S TRIUMPHANT RETURN TO ONE OF HIS CLASSIC CO-CREATIONS." FANS HAD THEIR GUESSES. IT WAS "BLACK PANTHER." I MADE HIM INTO A GLOBE-SPANNING JET-SET ADVENTURER PLUNDERING THE TREASURES OF KING SOLOMON'S MINES, EVADING DEATH TRAPS, AND FOLLOWING CLUES TO FIND KING SOLOMON'S GOLDEN FROG.

KING SOLOMON'S FROG

KNOCK LETTERS STARTED SHOWING UP IN MY BOOKS' LETTER COLUMNS. IT WAS OUT OF THE ORDINARY AND IT SEEMED LIKE THE INTERNS PUTTING TOGETHER THE COLUMNS HAD AN AXE TO GRIND. THE LETTER WRITERS KEPT SUGGESTING I TEAM UP WITH A WRITER AND THAT I CONNECT MY BOOKS WITH THE REST OF THE MARVEL LINE. AFTER MY EXPERIENCES WITH "SUPERMAN" I COULD ONLY SEE THE DOWNSIDE OF COORDINATING WITH OTHER BOOKS.

that the quality of Jack's recent w
--for Jack. I would like to see either
al influence or a writer who could wo

y, the times have changed. Altho
called the King, it wasn't until the

I WAS IN CALIFORNIA, FAR FROM THE MARVEL OFFICES IN NEW YORK. THERE WASN'T A LOT I COULD DO. STEVE SHERMAN'S BROTHER GARY PHONED ME WITH A QUESTION.

HOW WOULD YOU LIKE TO MEET PAUL MCCARTNEY?

HOW ABOUT GUY LOMBARDO?

ONE THING...I TOLD THEM A LITTLE WHITE LIE. PAUL DID A SONG "MAGNETO VS. THE TITANIUM MAN." I TOLD THEM YOU DID A DRAWING OF PAUL AND THE BAND WITH MAGNETO. CAN YOU WHIP A DRAWING UP IN AN HOUR?

I CAN DO THAT NO PROBLEM. MY KIDS WILL BE SO EXCITED.

WE WERE ON HOLIDAY AND YOUR COMIC BOOKS GAVE THE KIDS SOMETHING TO KEEP THEM OCCUPIED.

THERE'S SOMEBODY SPECIAL IN THE AUDIENCE TONIGHT. JACK COLBY.

JACK KIRBY.

ROY THOMAS CALLED ME ABOUT "FF."

JACK, I KNOW YOU DON'T WANT TO DO "FANTASTIC FOUR," BUT HOW ABOUT THIS ONE-OFF: "WHAT IF THE FANTASTIC FOUR WAS REALLY THE MARVEL BULLPEN?"

YOU'D BE THE THING. STAN WOULD BE MISTER FANTASTIC. FLO STEINBERG COULD BE SUE, AND I'D BE JOHNNY STORM.

I'LL DO IT, BUT ONLY IF I WRITE THE SCRIPT.

I DID THE COMIC. I KEPT IT TRUE TO MY EXPERIENCE. YOU COULDN'T LEAVE SOL BRODSKY OUT. HE WAS THE MARVEL BULLPEN. I DIDN'T REALLY HAVE MANY DEALINGS WITH ROY THOMAS BACK THEN SO SOL GOT THE ROLE AS HUMAN TORCH, NOT ROY.

GOT HIM, STAN! I'LL FLAME ON, AND—

NO YOU DON'T! HE'S MINE!

WELL, SO DO SOMETH TRYING TO

IT WAS FUN--NOSTALGIC, BUT I GOT TO TALK ABOUT WHAT THOSE YEARS WERE LIKE FOR ME--THE FRUSTRATIONS.

YOU ALWAYS DO IT AT THE WRONG TIME, THAT'S WHY!

WELL, GOOD FIGHTS DON'T GROW ON TREES, YA KNOW! THIS ONE COULD BE A CLASSIC, IF YOU'D ONLY STAY OUT OF IT!

WITH "ETERNALS" I WAS BUILDING AN EPIC LIKE "NEW GODS," BUT INSTEAD OF HAVING 80 PAGES A MONTH I HAD 17. I FILLED IT TO THE BRIM WITH CONCEPTS.

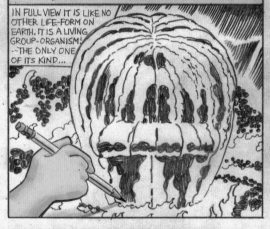

IN FULL VIEW IT IS LIKE NO OTHER LIFE-FORM ON EARTH. IT IS A LIVING GROUP-ORGANISM! --THE ONLY ONE OF ITS KIND...

I KEPT GETTING PRESSURE FROM THE OFFICE TO LINK IT TO THE MARVEL UNIVERSE, BUT I WAS CREATING MY OWN UNIVERSE, BASED ON TODAY, NOT NOSTALGIA FOR THE OLD COMICS I DID. I THREW IN S.H.I.E.L.D. AGENTS TO THROW THEM A BONE, BUT THAT WASN'T ENOUGH.

A-AFTER WHAT WE'VE SEEN HERE, MY MEN AND I MUST GET BACK TO SHIELD STARTING NOW!

A TV SHOW BASED ON "THE HULK" CAME OUT. IT WAS A HUGE HIT. I DIDN'T GET ANY CREDIT OR ANY MONEY.

I DID GET INVITED TO BE AN EXTRA ON THE SHOW. I PLAYED A POLICE SKETCH ARTIST, DRAWING THE HULK-- A ROLE I WAS BORN TO PLAY.

SALES ON "ETERNALS" WERE SLIPPING. THEY WANTED ME TO HAVE THE HULK SHOW UP IN IT. I DIDN'T WANT TO DO IT, BUT I PLAYED BALL.

I MADE IT A ROBOT HULK. OTHER COMICS ARE IN THE MARVEL UNIVERSE, MINE TAKE PLACE IN THE REAL WORLD. COMICS FANS BUILD A ROBOT THAT COMES TO LIFE. EDITORIAL DIDN'T PUSH THE ISSUE AFTER THAT. IT THREW THE PLOT OFF THE RAILS. IT TOOK ME A FEW ISSUES TO GET IT BACK ON TRACK.

THE KNOCK LETTERS KEPT FILLING UP THE LETTER COLUMNS AND IT WAS HURTING SALES. HOW COULD IT NOT? IMAGINE A BOOK THAT SAYS, "THIS BOOK YOU'RE READING STINKS, AND YOU'RE AN IDIOT FOR BUYING IT."

Dear People,
    The problem, put simply, is that Jack Kirby
comics. His art is just fine. There's nothing
plots. It's just his scripting. Oh, he has other
something could be done about his scripting, I'd
    So why is Kirby a law unto himself? Why i
years of Cap's life? Why sacrifice logic and rea
of action? Why?

WRITER AFTER WRITER AT MARVEL PETITIONED TO WRITE FOR ME, SO THEY COULD BE THE NEXT STAN LEE. SOME OF THESE WRITERS WERE WRITING THE LETTERS. SOME WERE ASSEMBLING THE LETTER COLUMNS. I COULDN'T STAY QUIET. I TOLD THE ONE PERSON IN THE COMPANY WHO I THOUGHT MIGHT UNDERSTAND--A PEER FROM MY GENERATION.

STANLEY, THEY'RE KILLING ME. *THIS IS SABOTAGE*

GOD, JACK. THIS HAS GOT TO STOP. I'M SORRY.

STAN TOOK CARE OF IT. THE POISON PEN LETTERS STOPPED. THE MAIL WAS REROUTED TO MY P.O. BOX IN THOUSAND OAKS. I EDITED THE LETTER COLUMNS FOR MY BOOKS IN-HOUSE.

HANDLING THE LETTER COLUMNS MYSELF DIDN'T SAVE "ETERNALS" FROM CANCELLATION.

I HAD TO FACE SOME HARD FACTS.

I WASN'T A YOUNG MAN ANY MORE. I WASN'T EVEN A MIDDLE-AGED MAN ANY MORE. COMICS IS A YOUNG MAN'S GAME. THE KIDS WERE DOING THEIR THING. DID I HAVE ANYTHING TO SAY THAT THE KIDS WANTED TO HEAR?

I DIDN'T WANT TO WORK ON "FF" OR "THOR." I DIDN'T WANT TO GO BACK IN TIME. I DIDN'T WANT TO TIE STUFF INTO THEIR MARVEL UNIVERSE. I WAS STARTING TO FEEL LIKE MAYBE THERE WASN'T A PLACE FOR ME AT MARVEL. THERE SURE WASN'T A PLACE FOR ME AT DC. I'D HIT THE LIMIT OF WHAT YOU CAN GET FROM A TWO-COMPANY INDUSTRY.

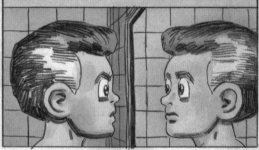

A YOUNG FILMMAKER, GEORGE LUCAS, WANTED MARVEL TO DO A COMIC BASED ON HIS UPCOMING SCI-FI MOVIE. HE MET WITH ROY THOMAS TO DISCUSS IT. MY NAME WAS MENTIONED.

THERE WAS A "SILVER SURFER" FILM IN THE WORKS. THEY APPROACHED ME ABOUT TEAMING UP WITH STANLEY ONE MORE TIME TO DO A GRAPHIC NOVEL THAT WOULD BE THE BASIS FOR THE FILM. SIMON AND SCHUSTER WOULD PUBLISH IT. IT WASN'T THE COMICS GHETTO. IT WAS A REAL PUBLISHER.

UH-HUH.

I SWORE I'D NEVER WORK WITH A WRITER AGAIN, AND DEFINITELY NOT WITH STANLEY.

IT CAN'T BE "WRITTEN BY STAN LEE, ART BY JACK KIRBY." IT'S GOT TO BE "COPYRIGHT STAN LEE AND JACK KIRBY."

IT WAS LEGITIMATE PUBLISHING. I GOT EQUAL CREDIT AND SHARED COPYRIGHT TO THE BOOK. IT WAS A REAL DEAL--A FIRST FOR ME, AND IT WOULD GET ME CLOSER TO CLOSING OUT MY MARVEL CONTRACT.

I WAS BACK WORKING WITH STANLEY AGAIN, BUT THIS TIME ON EQUAL FOOTING.

I CAME UP WITH A SCRIPT TREATMENT. I PUT EVERYTHING I HAD INTO IT, TYPOS AND ALL.

I SENT THE TREATMENT TO STANLEY. BEFORE LONG I REMEMBERED WHY I COULDN'T WORK WITH HIM. HE ADDED A BUNCH OF NONSENSE AND GARBAGE TO IT. HE MISSED THE POINT OF THE STORY.

HE UNDERMINED IT WITH THE NONSENSICAL BACKSTORY HE CAME UP WITH FOR THE SURFER BACK IN THE SIXTIES. MY SURFER IS AN ANGEL, A BEING OF PURE ENERGY CREATED BY THE HAND OF GOD. STANLEY'S WAS JUST ANOTHER COMIC BOOK SCIENTIST FROM A DOOMED PLANET.

JIM SHOOTER TOOK OVER AS MARVEL'S EDITOR-IN-CHIEF. HE GOT HIS START AT AGE 14, WRITING "LEGION OF SUPER-HEROES" COMICS FOR DC IN THE SIXTIES.

JACK, I WANT YOU TO COME UP WITH SOMETHING WE COULD ADAPT FOR SATURDAY MORNING TELEVISION.

THERE WAS A SHOW ON, "LAND OF THE LOST," WITH KIDS, DINOSAURS, AND MONOLITHS--AND A FURRY CAVE BOY LIKE MOONWATCHER IN ARTHUR CLARKE'S "2001." IF THAT'S WHAT SATURDAY MORNING TV WAS, I FELT RIGHT AT HOME.

I CAME UP WITH "DEVIL DINOSAUR" AND MOONBOY. IT'S A BOY AND HIS DOG, BUT HIS DOG IS A T. REX.

THE TV SHOW NEVER HAPPENED, BUT I GOT THE OPPORTUNITY TO WORK IN ANIMATION, DOING STORYBOARDS FOR A "FANTASTIC FOUR" CARTOON. THEY GAVE ME WIDE CREATIVE LATITUDE-- UNHEARD OF IN TV ANIMATION.

THERE WAS ONE CATCH. THEY DIDN'T HAVE CLEARANCE FOR THE HUMAN TORCH. HIS RIGHTS WERE TIED UP AT UNIVERSAL FOR A TV PILOT, SO I CREATED HIS REPLACEMENT, HERBIE, AN R2-D2 CHARACTER CROSSED WITH "HERBIE THE LOVE BUG."

HEY WHADDYA THINK YER DOIN'?

"OH, NO! NOT AGAIN!"

I'D ALWAYS FOUND THE ANIMATION INDUSTRY TOO CREATIVELY LIMITING, BUT THIS WAS DIFFERENT. THEY WANTED ME TO DO IT LIKE I DID WITH MY COMICS, PLOTTING ON THE FLY, BUT WITH MUCH BETTER PAY.

THEY GOT STANLEY TO WRITE A PLOT SYNOPSIS AND PUT IN THE DIALOGUE. THEY WANTED TO CAPTURE LIGHTNING IN A BOTTLE. THE PRODUCERS WERE A NEW GENERATION, KIDS WHO GREW UP ON MY COMICS. THEY WANTED US TO DO IT "MARVEL METHOD." I PUT MY NOTES IN THE MARGINS LIKE I DID IN THE SIXTIES.

BEN ROLLS REED INTO BALL

AIMS IT AT CAR

COMICS HAD NO ROYALTIES, NO PROFIT PARTICIPATION, BUT BOOK PUBLISHING DID. ANIMATION HAD HEALTH INSURANCE. I WASN'T HAVING THE CREATIVE FREEDOM AT COMICS THAT I ONCE HAD.

MAYBE ANIMATION IS MY WAY OUT OF COMICS.

ROZ AND I SAW "STAR WARS."

THIS SEEMS RIGHT UP YOUR ALLEY.

MAYBE TOO MUCH. THAT'S DOCTOR DOOM UP THERE.

THERE WAS A "SUPERMAN" FILM ON THE WAY AND NEAL ADAMS WAS GETTING SIEGEL AND SHUSTER IN FRONT OF REPORTERS, TELLING THEIR STORY OF HOW THEY CREATED SUPERMAN AND GOT SCREWED. I DIDN'T WANT TO END UP LIKE THEM, BUT THIS IS WHAT HAPPENS WHEN YOU CREATE A MEGAHIT IN COMICS. I COULDN'T STAY IN AN INDUSTRY LIKE THAT.

AFTER THE "FF" CARTOON I DID SOME FREELANCE WORK FOR HANNA-BARBERA ON THE "SUPERFRIENDS." MY OLD ASSISTANT MARK EVANIER SUGGESTED ME FOR A JOB AT ANOTHER ANIMATION COMPANY, RUBY-SPEARS.

WHEN I DROPPED MY WORK OFF IN THE OFFICE, THE YOUNG ARTISTS AND WRITERS THERE WERE JAZZED TO SEE ME.

KEN SPEARS OFFERED ME A FULL-TIME JOB.

HOW WOULD YOU LIKE TO COME WORK FOR US?

THE TIMING COULDN'T HAVE BEEN BETTER. I WAS GETTING OLD. DOCTOR VISITS WERE EXPENSIVE. THEY WERE OFFERING ME HEALTH COVERAGE AND PAID VACATIONS FOR THE FIRST TIME IN MY LIFE.

IN COMICS I WAS TREATED LIKE AN UNWANTED OLD MAN. THE OLD GRAY MARE, A BROKEN DOWN WARHORSE. IN ANIMATION I WAS BEING TREATED WITH RESPECT AND ADMIRATION.

OKAY, SEE IF YOU CAN FOLLOW THIS. I WAS HIRED TO DO DESIGN WORK FOR A SCI-FI MOVIE CALLED "LORD OF LIGHT."

THE C.I.A. BOUGHT THE RIGHTS AND CHANGED THE NAME OF THE PRODUCTION TO "ARGO" AND USED IT AS A COVER STORY TO RESCUE SIX U.S. DIPLOMATS DURING THE IRAN HOSTAGE CRISIS. THEY PUT TOGETHER A WHOLE FAKE MOVIE CREW AND PRETENDED TO SCOUT FILMING LOCATIONS IN IRAN WHILE GETTING THE DIPLOMATS OUT OF THE COUNTRY. TRUTH IS STRANGER THAN FICTION.

THE CAMPAIGN NEAL ADAMS STARTED TO GET CREDIT AND A PENSION FOR SIEGEL AND SHUSTER SUCCEEDED. THINGS WERE STARTING TO TURN IN THE RIGHT DIRECTION FOR CREATORS WITH SOME HELP FROM THIS YOUNGER, MORE OUTSPOKEN GENERATION.

GREG THEAKSTON USED TO BE AN ASSISTANT TO JIM STERANKO. HE OFFERED HIS SERVICES TO ME.

THESE PHOTOCOPIES SHOULD BE ARCHIVED. THIS IS COMICS HISTORY.

GO FOR IT.

HE INTERVIEWED ME--GOT ME TO TELL ALL THE OLD WAR STORIES. I LET HIM PUBLISH THE INTERVIEWS ALONG WITH MY OLD UNPUBLISHED COMICS AND ARTWORK. HE WAS CREATING A HISTORY OF JACK KIRBY.

THE S.S. TROOPERS CAME BURSTING INTO THE ROOM LIKE AN ERROL FLYNN MOVIE.

DAVE STEVENS, BEFORE HE CREATED "THE ROCKETEER," ASKED FOR ADVICE.

DON'T TRY TO DRAW LIKE ANYBODY ELSE. DO THINGS YOUR OWN WAY.

I WAS WORKING FULL TIME IN ANIMATION, BUT I WORKED ON SIDE PROJECTS. I WAS APPROACHED BY A COUPLE OF INVESTORS WHO WANTED TO START UP A "KIRBY COMICS" LINE. I PROPOSED A COMIC BOOK VERSION OF MY "CAPTAIN VICTORY" TREATMENT, A BIGFOOT COMIC CALLED "THUNDERFOOT", AND THE SUPERHEROES FROM HELL, "SATAN'S SIX." I WAS ALSO WORKING ON AN ONGOING OBSESSION, MY PROSE NOVEL, "THE HORDE."

JACK KIRBY COMICS PRESENT

LAST OF THE HALF HUMANS

IT WAS BASED ON A RECURRING NIGHTMARE ABOUT AN UNSTOPPABLE WAVE OF HUMANITY. THE THING IS, THE STUFF I WAS WRITING IN MY NOVEL STARTED HAPPENING IN REAL LIFE. IT HAPPENED ENOUGH TIMES THAT I GOT SCARED AND STOPPED WRITING IT.

I WORKED ON THE CARTOON "THUNDARR THE BARBARIAN." STEVE GERBER, THE CREATOR OF HOWARD THE DUCK, CAME UP WITH THE STORY. ALEX TOTH DESIGNED THE THREE MAIN CHARACTERS, BUT HAD OTHER COMMITMENTS AND COULDN'T CONTINUE WORK ON THE SHOW. I TOOK OVER AND CAME UP WITH THE DESIGNS FOR THE VILLAINS, CREATURES, SUPPORTING CHARACTERS, LOCATIONS, VEHICLES, AND SOME STORY IDEAS.

"THUNDARR" WAS A HIT. I LIKED BEING PART OF THE WHOLE PROCESS, SEEING IT THROUGH FROM PITCH TO EXECUTION.

WE PITCHED A "WONDER WOMAN" CARTOON.

IT NEVER MADE IT TO THE AIR.

WE DID A CARTOON ABOUT MR. T. IN REAL LIFE, HE STARTED OUT AS A BODYGUARD TO THE RICH AND FAMOUS, SO I CAME UP WITH A STORY CONCEPT LIKE THE MOVIE "MY BODYGUARD" WHERE SOME KIDS HIRE MR. T TO PROTECT THEM FROM BULLIES. THE OLYMPICS WERE COMING UP, SO THE CONCEPT CHANGED TO MR. T GETTING INTO ADVENTURES ON A BUS TOUR WITH A TRAVELLING GROUP OF GYMNASTS.

WE DID A SHOW ABOUT A KID WHO TRANSFORMS INTO AN AUTOMOBILE, CALLED "CARY BECOMES A CAR."

WHEN IT MADE IT TO THE AIR IT WAS RENAMED "TURBO TEEN."

ROZ AND I WENT OUT TO THE SECOND "STAR WARS" MOVIE.

I AM YOUR FATHER!

SON OF A BITCH.

THIS WAS LIKE "NEW GODS"— LIKE DARKSEID AND ORION.

COMICS SPECIALTY SHOPS WERE POPPING UP ACROSS THE COUNTRY. ONE OF THE COMPANIES THAT DISTRIBUTED BOOKS TO THESE STORES, PACIFIC COMICS, WANTED TO PUBLISH THEIR OWN LINE OF FULL COLOR COMICS FOR THIS DIRECT MARKET. THEY ASKED IF I WOULD DO THE FIRST ONE.

MAYBE YOU COULD DO SOMETHING ALONG THE LINES OF "STAR WARS."

I DUSTED OFF "CAPTAIN VICTORY." I ADDED SOME "STAR WARS" ELEMENTS AND SOME "BATTLESTAR GALACTICA" ELEMENTS. IF THEY CAN RIP ME OFF, I CAN RIP THEM OFF.

I TIED IT UNOFFICIALLY INTO THE "NEW GODS" CONTINUITY AND WAS ABLE TO CLOSE THE BOOK ON THAT UNFINISHED STORY. ORION'S SON ESCAPES A POST APOCALYPTIC APOKOLIPS, RENAMED "HELLIKOST."

NEW GODS

CAPTAIN VICTORY

MY CO-WORKER STEVE GERBER WAS IN THE MIDDLE OF A LEGAL BATTLE WITH MARVEL OVER THE OWNERSHIP OF HIS CHARACTER HOWARD THE DUCK.

JACK, I'M WRITING A FUNDRAISER COMIC TO PAY MY LEGAL BILLS. IT'S CALLED "DESTROYER DUCK." IT'S ABOUT A LITTLE DUCK THAT GETS EXPLOITED BY A BIG CORPORATION. EVENTUALLY HE GETS REVENGE AND TURNS THE CHAIRMAN OF THE BOARD INTO HAMBURGER... DO YOU WANT TO DRAW IT? FOR FREE?

HA·HA·HA

SURE, SOUNDS LIKE FUN.

STEVE AND I HAD A LOT OF ANGER AND FRUSTRATION WITH MARVEL. THE COMIC WAS A CATHARTIC EXPERIENCE FOR US.

A FILM CREW FROM "ENTERTAINMENT TONIGHT" CAME TO MY HOUSE TO INTERVIEW ME IN MY STUDIO.

HOW MANY CHARACTERS HAVE YOU CREATED?

IT WOULD PROBABLY COME DOWN TO AN ARMY DIVISION.

I FILLED UP A SKETCHBOOK WITH DRAWINGS OF MY CHARACTERS AS A VALENTINE'S DAY GIFT FOR ROZ.

KAMANDI

AS I GOT OLDER, MY FAITH BECAME MORE AND MORE IMPORTANT TO ME. I TOOK A GREAT DEAL OF COMFORT IN IT.

WHO ARE YOU DRAWING?

IT'S MOSES.

TOYS "R" US

GRANDMA! GRANDPA! CAN I GET IRON MAN?

DID YOU KNOW YOUR GRANDPA CREATED IRON MAN AND THE REST OF HIS TEAM.

I SAW SHELVES AND SHELVES OF TOYS I CREATED AND DON'T GET CREDIT OR A DIME FROM. I STARTED TO SHAKE.

I'M GONNA GO WAIT IN THE CAR.

I WAS WORKING FULL-TIME IN ANIMATION, BUT JENETTE KAHN GAVE ME ANOTHER SHOT AT MY MAGNUM OPUS.

WE FEEL LIKE YOU WEREN'T TREATED FAIRLY THE FIRST TIME AROUND AT DC. "NEW GODS" WAS A MASTERPIECE, BUT THE OLD REGIME DIDN'T KNOW WHAT THEY HAD. WE DO.

THE NEW GODS ARE GOING TO BE INCORPORATED INTO THE "SUPERFRIENDS" SATURDAY MORNING CARTOON, AND IT'S GOING TO BE COORDINATED WITH A LINE OF ACTION FIGURES.

WE WANT TO GIVE YOU THE OPPORTUNITY TO FINISH YOUR "NEW GODS" STORY THE WAY THEY SHOULD'VE LET YOU. WE CAN OFFER YOU THE SAME CREATOR ROYALTY WE OFFER NOW. WE'LL REPRINT THE OLD STORIES AND THEN FOLLOW IT UP WITH YOUR NEW CONCLUSION.

WE'LL GRANDFATHER YOU IN, BUT TO JUSTIFY IT TO WARNER BROTHERS WE WANT YOU TO DESIGN THE NEW TOYS. YOU'LL GET A ROYALTY ON EVERY DARKSEID DOLL, EVERY MISTER MIRACLE DOLL--ALL OF IT.

I'LL FINALLY BE ABLE TO SHOW MY FACE AT TOYS "R" US.

SO I ADDED TOY DESIGNER TO MY RESUMÉ. I LOVED IT. I CAME UP WITH ALL KINDS OF GIMMICKS FOR THE FIGURINES.

THE SAN DIEGO COMIC-CON STARTED A COMICS AWARD CEREMONY. THEY CALLED THEM "THE JACK KIRBY COMICS INDUSTRY AWARDS" AND I OFFICIATED.

CONGRATULATIONS, KID.

AT THAT SAME CONVENTION, THERE WAS A MARVEL 25TH ANNIVERSARY PARTY.

JACK! YOU LOOK GREAT! HOW'VE YOU BEEN?

NOT BAD, STANLEY. IT'S GOOD TO SEE YOU.

YOU KNOW, JACK...I DON'T CARE WHO OWNS THE CHARACTERS. I DON'T CARE WHO GETS THE CREDIT. YOU CAN OWN IT, YOU CAN HAVE ALL THE CREDIT. I JUST WANT TO WORK WITH YOU ONE MORE TIME.

YEAH, I'D LIKE THAT, TOO.

OVER MY DEAD BODY.

HEY! SEE THIS GUY I DREW? WELL HE'S NOT A "ROOF-JUMPER" IN AN ART-DECO SUIT!--NOR IS HE THE MASTER MAGOO IN SOME OPUS WITH A FIFTEEN DOLLAR CONCLUSION! THIS GUY IS THE END OF THE WORLD! THIS GUY IS HOLOCAUST WITH A BIG "H"!

I'M JACK KIRBY! I'LL SHOW YOU THE NEW GODS AS THEY REALLY ARE!

I TOLD THE STORY OF THE LAST DAYS OF THE WAR OF THE GODS. THERE WAS A LOSS OF INNOCENCE. JUST AS OUR WORLD HAS CHANGED SINCE THE SIXTIES, SO TOO HAD APOKOLIPS AND NEW GENESIS--THEY BECAME COMPUTERIZED AND DEHUMANIZED. IF YOU THOUGHT HELL COULDN'T GET ANY WORSE, IT DID.

YOU'VE RIPPED OFF THE ANTI-LIFE EQUATION.

SIRE! BEHOLD, THE MICRO-MARK!

FACE-- I--I--

THE SOURC MADE US--

OH, GREAT SOURCE! SHOW HIM KINDNESS IN HIS PASSING! JUDGE HIM AS HE WAS AND NOT AS HE BECAME!

SEE HIM NOT AS A BITTER PAWN SUR-PRISED IN FATAL DEFEAT, BUT ONLY AS A CHILD, FALLEN UPON CRUEL DAYS...

THERE WAS STILL THE POSSIBILITY OF REDEMPTION AND A RECLAMATION OF YOUR OWN HUMANITY THROUGH THE SOURCE AND ITS MYSTERIES.

DICK GIORDANO AND DC EDITORIAL DIDN'T LIKE IT. THEY WANTED ME TO SUM UP THE STORY OF THE NEW GODS IN 24 PAGES, BUT THAT JUST WASN'T ENOUGH. I TOLD THE STORY HONESTLY AND THE WAY I SAW IT.

WE'VE BEEN HAVING A LOT OF SUCCESS WITH THE GRAPHIC NOVEL FORMAT. WHY DON'T YOU ADD SOME PAGES TO THIS AND WE'LL PUT IT OUT AS A DELUXE GRAPHIC NOVEL?

I CAME UP WITH MORE PAGES. I SHOWED HOW NEW GENESIS WAS CHANGING, THE OTHER SIDE OF THE COIN. IT ENDED WITH ORION RESCUING HIS MOTHER TIGRA AND LEAVING DARKSEID TO LIVE OUT HIS REMAINING YEARS ALONE AND DEPOSED.

I CREATED A COLLAGE FOR THE DESTRUCTION OF NEW GENESIS, HOME OF THE HEROIC GODS. I CUT UP ONE OF MY BELOVED PULPS FOR IT. THAT'S HOW MUCH THIS COMIC MEANT TO ME.

JACK, THIS ISN'T EXACTLY WHAT WE ADVERTISED. WE PROMISED THE FANS A BIG EXPLOSIVE FIGHT BETWEEN FATHER AND SON, LIKE "STAR WARS," AND LIKE YOU FORESHADOWED IN THE OLD SERIES. WE DON'T WANT TO LIE TO THE READERS.

ARE YOU CALLING ME A LIAR, DICK?

SO I GAVE THEM A BIG BATTLE. I'M A FATHER. I COULDN'T IMAGINE A FATHER, EVEN DARKSEID, PERFORMING THE COUP DE GRACE ON HIS OWN SON, SO DARKSEID LURED ORION INTO A TRAP WHERE HIS EXECUTIONER SQUAD DID THE DEED.

MARKSMEN, AND VITAL TARGETS!

THE PROBLEM IS WE WANT TO MAKE TOYS FROM THESE CHARACTERS SO YOU NEED TO MAKE SURE EVERYBODY'S STILL ALIVE BY THE END OF IT, INCLUDING THE CHARACTERS YOU KILLED IN THE ORIGINAL SERIES.

≷GROAN≷

I SAW THE RESULTS OF THE "HUNGER DOGS" GRAPHIC NOVEL. IT WAS FAR FROM WHAT I'D ENVISIONED, BUT I STAND BY IT.

I WAS TELLING STORIES ABOUT MY CHILDHOOD IN THE GHETTO. RICHARD KYLE WAS STARTING A NEW MAGAZINE CALLED "ARGOSY" AND ASKED ME TO DRAW THE STORY I JUST TOLD HIM.

YOU WANT IT JUST THE WAY IT WAS?

JUST THE WAY IT WAS. I'LL PRINT WHATEVER YOU DRAW.

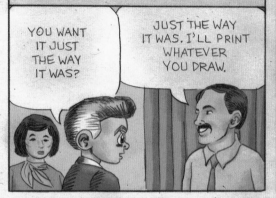

THE RESULT WAS "STREET CODE," ONE DAY IN THE LIFE OF YOUNG JACOB KURTZBERG, FEATURING THE POVERTY, THE VIOLENCE, THE RITUALS AND EXHILARATION OF MY CHILDHOOD.

STOP IT! IF YOU WANT A HOT ROLL, ASK ME!

YOU GONNA MAKE MORE, MOM?

THE 3-D FAD WAS MAKING A COMEBACK. THEY WERE SHOWING OLD 3-D MOVIES ON TV WITH GLASSES YOU COULD GET AT 7-ELEVEN. I DID SOME 3-D COMICS WITH A FELLOW NAMED RAY ZONE WHO WAS INTERESTED IN STEREO-OPTICS.

THE COMIC CAME PACKAGED WITH 3-D GLASSES THAT SAID "JACK KIRBY: KING OF COMICS."

JOHNNY CARSON WAS DOING A 3-D BIT ON HIS SHOW. WHAT DO YOU KNOW--HE WAS USING A PAIR OF MY 3-D GLASSES.

WHAT'S THIS SAY? "JACK KIRBY: KING OF COMICS?" ED, HAVE YOU EVER HEARD OF A JACK KIRBY?

I KNOW EVERY STAND-UP COMIC IN THE BUSINESS. I'VE NEVER HEARD OF JACK KIRBY. "KING OF THE COMICS?" MORE LIKE "KING OF THE CONMEN."

MARK EVANIER OFFERED TO CALL UP CARSON'S PRODUCER. JOHNNY DID A FULL RETRACTION AND TALKED IN GLOWING TERMS ABOUT MY WORK.

ONE NIGHT I WAS INVITED TO A DINNER PARTY AT BILLY MUMY'S HOUSE. BILLY HAD PLAYED WILL ROBINSON ON "LOST IN SPACE." I KNEW HIM FROM THE COMIC-CON CIRCUIT. JERRY SIEGEL WAS THERE, BOB KANE, THE ACTOR MIGUEL FERRER FROM "ROBOCOP," AND MARK HAMILL.

THE YOUNG "STAR WARS" ACTOR WAS WELL-VERSED IN THE LORE OF COMICS. I WAS ALWAYS AT A LOSS WHEN I TALKED TO SOMEONE LIKE THAT. THEY HAVE A RECOLLECTION OF THE INS AND OUTS OF MY WORK THAT I DON'T HAVE.

BOB KANE HAD CHANGED A LOT FROM THE YOUNG KID I KNEW IN THE OLD DAYS. HE SEEMED CYNICAL AND STANDOFFISH HE WAS CONSTANTLY BRAGGING AND PUTTING PEOPLE DOWN. HE HAD A LAUGH JUST LIKE THE PENGUIN.

AT SAN DIEGO I MET PETER LAIRD AND KEVIN EASTMAN, CREATORS OF THE "TEENAGE MUTANT NINJA TURTLES."

THEY WERE FANS AND BOUGHT SEVERAL PAGES OF MY ORIGINAL ART.

YOU'RE GOING TO HAVE TO TAKE IT EASY FROM NOW ON.

I DON'T WANT ANYBODY TO KNOW ABOUT THIS.

IF WORD GETS OUT, THEY'LL STOP GIVING ME WORK. I DON'T WANT TO BE PUT OUT TO PASTURE.

THE HEALTH INSURANCE FROM MY ANIMATION JOB SAVED MY LIFE. I TOOK ON ANOTHER COMICS GIG. IT WAS "SUPER POWERS" BASED ON THE TOYS I DESIGNED.

I DID MY BEST, BUT I COULDN'T DO COMICS ANY MORE. ALL THOSE TINY DRAWINGS WERE TOO MUCH.

I TRIED TO GET MY ARTWORK BACK FROM MARVEL. IT WAS BASICALLY SITTING OUT IN THE OPEN IN A HALLWAY THERE. PEOPLE WERE STEALING IT.

LAWYERS WERE INVOLVED. MARVEL SAID THEY'D GIVE ME THE ART BACK, BUT ONLY IF I SIGNED AWAY ALL MY RIGHTS, INCLUDING THE RIGHT TO TELL MY GRANDCHILDREN THAT I CREATED CAPTAIN AMERICA, THE HULK, FF, X-MEN, AVENGERS, ETC. MARVEL TOLD ME 99% OF MY PAGES WERE "MISSING."

MARVEL TOLD ME THEY HAD 88 OF MY PAGES. I DID THOUSANDS OF PAGES FOR THEM.

THEY SENT ME A CONTRACT THEY SAID I HAD TO SIGN IF I WANTED ANY ARTWORK BACK. ONE OF THE CLAUSES SAID I WASN'T ALLOWED TO TELL ANYONE, NOT EVEN MY CHILDREN, THAT I CREATED THOSE CHARACTERS. IT WAS TOO MUCH.

ON THE BACK OF MY PAYCHECK, THEY'D WRITE THIS LONG CONTRACT. BY SIGNING THE BACK OF YOUR CHECK, YOU WERE SIGNING THIS VERKAKTE CONTRACT. I COULDN'T UNDERSTAND IT. I SHOWED IT TO MY WIFE, MY KIDS, MY LAWYER. NOBODY COULD BELIEVE IT.

I DIDN'T HAVE TO BE AFRAID OF THEM TAKING AWAY MY LIVELIHOOD. I WASN'T DEPENDENT ON THEM ANY MORE.

YOUNG CARTOONISTS TOOK UP MY CAUSE AND USED IT TO PUSH FOR CREATOR RIGHTS ACROSS THE BOARD. THE BIG COMPANIES STARTED GIVING CREATORS ROYALTIES AND HEALTH INSURANCE.

A CAPTAIN AMERICA MOVIE WAS COMING. THE POSTERS SAID "BASED ON THE CHARACTER CREATED BY STAN LEE." I CALLED MY LAWYER.

Based on the character created by Stan Lee

MR. KIRBY, COULD YOU DRAW CAPTAIN AMERICA FOR ME?

I HURT MY HAND, SO I'M NOT DRAWING TODAY. WILL THIS DO?

I HATED TO LIE TO THE KID, BUT I DIDN'T WANT WORD GETTING OUT THAT AFTER MY ATTACK I COULDN'T DRAW LIKE I USED TO.

ROZ AND I WENT TO THE HOLY LAND, MY FIRST EVER VACATION. I LEFT A NOTE IN THE WESTERN WALL.

WHAT DID IT SAY?

"THANKS FOR THE VACATION."

MY LAWYER GOT MY NAME ON THE CAPTAIN AMERICA MOVIE. JOE'S NAME WAS UP THERE, TOO. I GOT INVITED TO THE MOVIE PREMIERE. IT WAS A STINKER--A B-PICTURE. THE RED SKULL WASN'T A NAZI, HE WAS ITALIAN. CAP KEPT HIS COSTUME HIDDEN UNDER A TRENCHCOAT FOR MOST OF THE MOVIE.

I SHOULD CALL MY LAWYER AND GET MY NAME TAKEN OFF OF IT.

IT WASN'T LONG BEFORE THE NICETIES WORE AWAY.

EVERY WORD OF DIALOGUE IN THOSE SCRIPTS WERE MINE.

I WROTE A FEW LINES MYSELF ABOVE EVERY PANEL.

THEY WEREN'T PRINTED IN THE BOOKS.

I WASN'T ALLOWED TO WRITE.

I DON'T THINK YOU EVER READ ONE OF MY BOOKS AFTER IT WAS FINISHED. YOU WERE TOO BUSY DRAWING THE NEXT ONE.

KEVIN EASTMAN OF NINJA TURTLES FAME PUBLISHED "THE ART OF JACK KIRBY" BY RAY WYMAN. MAYBE MY WORK WOULD OUTLIVE ME AFTER ALL.

I WAS ON A NEW YORK RADIO SHOW HONORING MY 70TH BIRTHDAY.

JACK, WE HAVE A SURPRISE GUEST ON THE PHONE. GOOD MORNING, STAN.

I WANT TO WISH JACK A HAPPY BIRTHDAY. IT'S A HELLUVA COINCIDENCE. I'M IN NEW YORK. I WAS TUNING IN THE RADIO AND I HEARD JACK TALKING ABOUT MARVEL AND I COULDN'T LET THE OCCASION GO BY.

THE FOLKS AT SAN DIEGO COMIC-CON THREW ME A SURPRISE BIRTHDAY PARTY. PROS LIKE FRANK MILLER WERE IN ATTENDANCE.

HAPPY BIRTHDAY TO...
JACK KIRBY
KING OF THE COMIC BOOKS

A GROUP OF YOUNG MARVEL ARTISTS LEFT AND STARTED THEIR OWN COMICS COMPANY. THEY WERE FANS OF MY WORK.

image

I DID A COMIC CALLED "PHANTOM FORCE" WITH MIKE THIBODEAUX, MY INKER ON "CAPTAIN VICTORY." IT WAS FRANKENSTEINED OUT OF OLD COMICS THAT NEVER GOT OFF THE GROUND.

IT INCLUDED A BRUCE LEE COMIC I DID ON SPEC DURING THE KUNG FU MOVIE CRAZE. THE BITS AND PIECES WERE YEARS APART. AT THIS POINT I WASN'T DRAWING ANY MORE. MIKE WAS GHOSTING FOR ME.

MIKE HAD INKED "PHANTOM FORCE" ON OVERLAYS SO THE PENCILLED ART WAS STILL INTACT. THE IMAGE GUYS WANTED TO INK THE PAGES THEMSELVES, DIRECTLY ON MY ORIGINAL ART. THEY WANTED A CHANCE TO COLLABORATE WITH ME, AND INKING ON AN OVERLAY JUST DIDN'T FEEL THE SAME.

AS PER THE IMAGE DEAL, ONCE THEY DEDUCTED THEIR STANDARD FEE, I GOT THE REMAINING PROFITS. IT WAS MY BIGGEST PAYCHECK EVER.

WHAT. D'YA KNOW?

THERE'S MONEY IN COMICS.

DECADES AFTER BREAKING INTO THE BUSINESS, I WAS RICH--FROM COMICS.

ONE OF THE IMAGE COMICS GUYS, ROB LIEFELD, CAME TO VISIT MY STUDIO. I SHOWED HIM MY TREASURE TROVE OF UNUSED ARTWORK. "PHANTOM FORCE" CAUGHT HIS ATTENTION.

I WANT TO PUBLISH THIS!

IT WASN'T MY BEST WORK, OR ANYBODY'S FINEST HOUR, BUT IT WAS GOOD ENOUGH. IT HAD THE SLICK GLOSSY PRODUCTION I'D ALWAYS WANTED FOR MY WORK.

SHORTLY AFTER THAT, THE COMICS BOOM WENT BUST. SALES ON ISSUE TWO WERE WAY BELOW THE FIRST ONE. THAT THAT WAS THAT.

I WAS ASKED TO BE ON BOB NEWHART'S NEW SHOW WHERE HE PLAYED A COMICS ARTIST. I PLAYED MYSELF.

TOPPS, THE BASEBALL CARD COMPANY, APPROACHED ME ABOUT DOING A WHOLE LINE OF COMICS. I PITCHED THEM "THE SECRET CITY SAGA."

I'M PRETTY MUCH RETIRED FROM DRAWING.

WE CAN GET OTHER PEOPLE TO WRITE AND DRAW THEM. WHAT WE WANT IS YOUR IMAGINATION AND IDEAS.

I DUG DEEP INTO THE ARCHIVES FOR ANY BIT THAT WAS USABLE. THE BOOKS WERE WRITTEN AND DRAWN BY TOP TALENT LIKE DITKO, GIFFEN, SIMONSON, AND ROY THOMAS. I WAS PAID VERY WELL FOR IT. IT SEEMS LIKE THE LESS WORK I DO ON A COMIC, THE MORE I GET PAID FOR IT IN THIS BRAVE NEW WORLD.

I WAS ON A PANEL DISCUSSING MARVEL'S REFUSAL TO RETURN MY ORIGINAL ART.

WHAT ADVANTAGES DO I THINK COMIC ARTIST'S HAVE? EVERYTHING WE DO WE CREATE WITH A PENCIL. HOLLYWOOD CAN'T KEEP UP WITH US. IF I WANT TO DESTROY OUR ENTIRE PLANET, I CAN DO IT WITH A DOUBLE-PAGE SPREAD AND IT COSTS ME MY PENCIL AND MY ERASER AND MY PAPER.

WHEN ALL WAS SAID AND DONE, I GOT MY ART BACK FROM MARVEL. IT WASN'T ANYWHERE CLOSE TO EVERYTHING, BUT A LOT MORE THAN THE 88 PAGES THEY TOLD ME AT FIRST.

DISNEY WANTED ME TO CONTRIBUTE TO AN ART BOOK THEY WERE DOING. MIKE THIBODEAUX HELPED ME FRANKENSTEIN A KIRBY-STYLE MICKEY MOUSE OUT OF AN OLD SKETCH.

I DIDN'T WANT ANYONE TO KNOW I COULD BARELY HOLD A PENCIL.

HE HELPED ME DO A SIMILAR THING FOR A "STAR WARS" TRADING CARD FOR TOPPS.

I CAN'T THANK YOU ENOUGH, MIKE.

MY CHILDHOOD FRIEND, LEON KLINGHOFFER, FROM THE BOYS BROTHERHOOD REPUBLIC DAYS, WAS ON A CRUISE OFF THE COAST OF EGYPT THAT WAS HIJACKED BY THE PALESTINE LIBERATION FRONT. HE WAS THE ONLY ONE THAT STOOD UP TO THEM. A GUY FROM MY BLOCK WOULD DO THAT.

THEY SHOT HIM AND THREW HIM OVERBOARD.

CHRISSIE HARPER STARTED A UK-BASED MAGAZINE, "THE JACK KIRBY QUARTERLY," FOCUSED ON MY LIFE AND WORK.

DID YOU HAVE ANY SPECIFIC PLAN FOR CAP OR "THE ETERNALS" BEFORE YOU LEFT MARVEL?

YES, I KNOW WHAT I WANTED TO DO WITH "ETERNALS," BUT IF CIRCUMSTANCES DON'T COME TO FRUITION, THEN THEY JUST COME TO A HALT.

I KEEP 'EM IN MY OWN HEAD. I KEEP ALL THE IDEAS IN MY OWN HEAD.

YOUR IDEAS BELONG TO YOU.

I HAD MY DRAWINGS OF GOD, MOSES, AND THE ANGELS—STORIES FROM THE BIBLE. THE DRAWINGS I'D DONE FOR FUN WERE BEING MADE INTO SCULPTURES, POSTERS, AND FINE ART PRINTS.

WE RENEWED OUR VOWS. THE WHOLE FAMILY WAS THERE—CHILDREN AND GRANDCHILDREN.

YOU WERE ALWAYS MY GREATEST COLLABORATOR.

February 6, 1994

NEW YORK TIMES
Jack Kirby, 76; Created Comic-Book Superheroes

THE NEW YORKER | HOMAGE TO JACK KIRBY BY GARY PANTER

YOU KNOW I ALWAYS THOUGHT DITKO WAS JACK'S BEST INKER.

AN AGE PASSES WITH JACK KIRBY. THERE IS BEFORE KIRBY AND AFTER KIRBY. ONE AGE DOES NOT RESEMBLE THE OTHER.

THE KING IS DEAD. THERE IS NO SUCCESSOR TO THAT TITLE. WE WILL NEVER SEE HIS LIKE AGAIN.

יעקב בן בנימין

Jack ♔ Kirby

Beloved Husband, Father and Grandfather

✡ 1917 — 1994

An Inspiration To All

THE *JACK KIRBY~* COLLECTOR

$2.50

ISSUE 10 SEPT 1994

FULLY AUTHORIZED BY THE KIRBY ESTATE

THIS IS OUR WORLD, UGLY, AND YOU WON'T GET IT WITHOUT A FIGHT.

GOODBYE, OLD FRIEND.

DEDICATED TO THE MEMORY OF
JACK KIRBY

SILVER SURFER

Silver Surfer Created By
JACK KIRBY
STAN LEE

WHY ISN'T MY NAME FIRST?

SILVER SURFER

Silver Surfer Created By
STAN LEE
JACK KIRBY

...THIS MACHINE DRAWS ITS POWER FROM MAGNETO...

THE PRODUCERS OF X-MEN WISH TO THANK THE FOLLOWING FOR THEIR ASSISTANCE

WESTCHESTER FILM OFFICE
GOODERHAM AND WORTS DISTILLERY
STATUE OF LIBERTY NATIONAL MONUMENT
TITAN MOTORCYCLES
STAN LEE
JACK KIRBY

SPIDER-MAN

DAREDEVIL

BASED ON THE MARVEL COMIC BOOK CHARACTER CREATED BY STAN LEE AND JACK KIRBY

I'M IRON MAN.

THIS COURT DETERMINES THAT IT WAS WORK MADE FOR HIRE AND THEREFORE MARVEL IS THE AUTHOR. JACK KIRBY'S HEIRS HAVE NO CLAIM TO THE CHARACTERS UNDER THE 1976 COPYRIGHT ACT.

Lisa Kirby, Neal Kirby, Susan Kirby and Barbara Kirby petition Supreme Court of the United States to hear historic case.

Marvel and the family of Jack Kirby have amicably resolved their legal disputes, and are looking forward to advancing their shared goal of honoring Mr. Kirby's significant role in Marvel's history.

AGENTS OF S.H.I.E.L.D.

INHUMANS BASED ON THE MARVEL COMICS BY STAN LEE AND JACK KIRBY

ANT-MAN BASED ON THE MARVEL COMICS BY STAN LEE AND JACK KIRBY

ACCEPTING THE DISNEY LEGENDS AWARD ON BEHALF OF HIS FATHER IS NEAL KIRBY.

DISNEY LEGEND JACK KIRBY

MY FATHER WOULD BE HUMBLED AND PROUD TO ACCEPT THIS AWARD. HE WAS PROBABLY THE MOST HUMBLE MAN ON THE FACE OF THE PLANET. THANK YOU FOR ENJOYING HIS INCREDIBLE AND STAGGERING BODY OF WORK...

BLACK PANTHER BASED ON THE MARVEL COMICS BY STAN LEE AND JACK KIRBY

HERE ARE THE FILMS SELECTED AS BEST PICTURE NOMINEES.

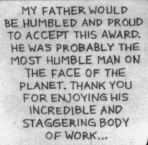

BLACK PANTHER...

AVENGERS ENDGAME

I CAN'T BEGIN TO DESCRIBE HOW MY FATHER WOULD FEEL SEEING HIS CHARACTERS ON THE SCREEN ALL AT ONCE WITH THE AVENGERS. HE SAW EVERY ONE OF HIS COMIC BOOKS BASICALLY AS A STORYBOARD FOR A MOVIE.

MARVEL STUDIOS
ETERNALS
BASED ON THE MARVEL COMICS BY
JACK KIRBY

NEW GODS
BASED ON THE DC COMICS BY
JACK KIRBY

I BEGAN TO ASK MYSELF, "EVERYBODY ELSE HAD THEIR GODS...WHO ARE OUR GODS?" WHAT IS THE SHAPE OF OUR SOCIETY IN THE FORM OF MYTH AND LEGEND? WHO ARE OUR EVIL GODS AND WHO ARE OUR GOOD ONES?

I'M A GUY WHO LIVES WITH A LOT OF QUESTIONS. I SAY "WHAT'S OUT THERE?" AND I TRY TO RESOLVE THAT AND I NEVER CAN. I DON'T THINK ANYONE CAN. WE CAN DO BETTER. WE WANNA DO BETTER. THE CHARACTERS REPRESENT A TRANSCENDANT FEELING THAT WE ALL HAVE INSIDE US.

I HAVEN'T GOT THE TRAPPINGS OF THE CIRCUS, BUT THERE IN MY MIND IS A VERY ACTIVE AND BRIGHT AND COLORFUL PLACE. NO MATTER WHAT KIND OF CHARACTER YOU CREATE OR ASSUME, A LITTLE OF YOURSELF MUST REMAIN THERE. IF YOU LOOK AT MY CHARACTERS, YOU'LL FIND ME.

THE END

NOTES

PAGE 2: *The Art of Jack Kirby*, by Ray Wyman. P 4.

PAGES 5–6: "She called on the rabbis and they all gathered around my bed and chanted in Hebrew: 'Demon, come out of this boy,' they said, 'What is your name, demon?'" *The Art of Jack Kirby*, by Ray Wyman. P 4.

PAGE 7: *The Art of Jack Kirby*, by Ray Wyman. P 5–8.

PAGE 8: "Everybody who lived on Suffolk Street would be the Suffolk Street Gang. Everybody who lived on Norfolk Street would be the Norfolk Street Gang." "I've Never Done Anything Half-Heartedly," by Gary Groth. *The Comics Journal Library: Jack Kirby*, edited by Milo George. May 2002.

PAGE 9: "You know, the punches were real, and the anger was real, and we'd chase each other up and down fire escapes, over rooftops, and we'd climb across clotheslines, and there were real injuries." "I've Never Done Anything Half-Heartedly," by Gary Groth. *The Comics Journal Library: Jack Kirby*, edited by Milo George. May 2002.

PAGE 12: "Hebrew school was a rough place. An airplane flew over one day and I ran over to the window and everyone was pushing and shoving each other, and some guy really shoved me out of the way—I knocked him clean out." "I've Never Done Anything Half-Heartedly," by Gary Groth. *The Comics Journal Library: Jack Kirby*, edited by Milo George. May 2002.

PAGE 13: "The House That Jack Built," by Glenn B. Fleming. *The Collected Jack Kirby Collector Volume Two*, edited by John Morrow. 1998. P 14.

PAGE 13: "Jack Kirby: An Artist with Impact," interview by Len Wein. *Jack Kirby Collector #49*. P 11.

PAGE 14: "The gangsters locked me in a telephone booth—I was about 9 years old." "Jack Kirby & Don Rico Discuss WWII, The Mafia, Watergate, & Comic Art," interview by Don Rico. *Jack Kirby Collector #20*, 1998. Originally published in *Mysticogryfil*, edited by Barry Alfonso.

PAGE 16: "I'd run errands for the reporters. My boss was playing golf [in the office], and he was shooting golf balls through an upturned telephone book, see?" "I've Never Done Anything Half-Heartedly," by Gary Groth. *The Comics Journal Library: Jack Kirby*, edited by Milo George. May 2002.

PAGE 17: "I saw the Marx brothers on a stage when they weren't even in the movies." "I've Never Done Anything Half-Heartedly," by Gary Groth. *The Comics Journal Library: Jack Kirby*, edited by Milo George. May 2002.

PAGE 17: "A friend of mine was shot and I saw the way his mother was after that." "The House That Jack Built," by Glenn B. Fleming. *The Collected Jack Kirby Collector Volume Two*, edited by John Morrow. 1998. P 15.

PAGE 20: "I was doing editorials. I did Your Health Comes First." "I've Never Done Anything Half-Heartedly," by Gary Groth. *The Comics Journal Library: Jack Kirby*, edited by Milo George. May 2002.

PAGE 22: "Superman saved my life." *Jack Kirby at War*, video interview, conducted March 17, 1983, filmed by Greg Theakston and Tony Dispoto, posted by The Jack Kirby Museum & Research Center on YouTube.

PAGE 26: *The Comic Book Makers*, by Joe Simon with Jim Simon. 1990. P 47.

PAGE 30: Joe Simon: "Robbie Solomon was there, as were Martin Goodman's three younger brothers, in descending order of age: Abe, Dave and Artie." "Simon Says! Joe Simon

On The Comic Book Biz, Jack Kirby, And A Few Other Things," by Jim Amash. *Alter Ego #76*, March 2008.

PAGE 35: Joe Simon: "Uncle Robbie brought him in and said 'This is Martin's nephew (or whatever he was). Can you find something for him to do?'" "Simon Says! Joe Simon On The Comic Book Biz, Jack Kirby, And A Few Other Things," by Jim Amash. *Alter Ego #76*, March 2008.

PAGE 37: "You know, he was the kind of kid that liked to fool around—open and close doors on you. Yeah. In fact, once I told Joe to throw him out of the room." "I've Never Done Anything Half-Heartedly," by Gary Groth. *The Comics Journal Library: Jack Kirby*, edited by Milo George. May 2002.

PAGE 38: "Would You Like To See My Etchings?" Interview with Roz Kirby by John Morrow. *The Collected Jack Kirby Collector Volume Two*, edited by John Morrow. 1998. P 40.

PAGE 39: Joe Simon: "They were outside and the police were there, and I did get a call from Mayor Fiorello LaGuardia." "Simon Says! Joe Simon On The Comic Book Biz, Jack Kirby, And A Few Other Things," by Jim Amash. *Alter Ego #76*, March 2008.

PAGES 39–40: *The Comic Book Makers*, by Joe Simon with Jim Simon. 1990. P 61.

PAGE 43: *The Comic Book Makers*, by Joe Simon with Jim Simon. 1990. P 62.

PAGE 45: Joe Simon: "Super Sherlock didn't work out so they gave us some of their other characters to do. It was a common thing to fix up other people's characters." "Simon Says! Joe Simon On The Comic Book Biz, Jack Kirby, And A Few Other Things," by Jim Amash. *Alter Ego #76*, March 2008.

PAGE 51: "Would You Like To See My Etchings?" Interview with Roz Kirby by John Morrow. *The Collected Jack Kirby Collector Volume Two*, edited by John Morrow. 1998. P 46.

PAGE 53: "I joined the Coast Guard because I had a chance to be with the horses in the Mounted Patrol." "Simon Says! Joe Simon On The Comic Book Biz, Jack Kirby, And A Few Other Things," by Jim Amash. *Alter Ego #76*, March 2008.

PAGE 53: "You get two free telegrams from the army: One to tell you you are drafted, one to tell your wife that you are coming home in a casket." "Jack Kirby on: World War II Influences Part Two," interview conducted by Ray Wyman, Jr. *Jack Kirby Collector #27*, February 2000.

PAGE 54: "My card was stamped NAVY." "Jack Kirby & Don Rico Discuss WW II, The Mafia, Watergate, & Comic Art," interview by Don Rico. *Jack Kirby Collector #20*, June 1998. Originally published in *Mysticogryfil*, edited by Barry Alfonso.

PAGE 55: "Fighting became second nature. I began to like it. And I love wrestling. When I went into the Army, I took judo. Out of a class of 27, just me and another fellow graduated." "I've Never Done Anything Half-Heartedly," by Gary Groth. *The Comics Journal Library: Jack Kirby*, edited by Milo George. May 2002.

PAGES 56–57: "Jack Kirby on: World War II Influences Part Two," interview conducted by Ray Wyman, Jr. *Jack Kirby Collector #27*, February 2000. P 18.

PAGES 58–59: "We were holding a brick factory and the SS troopers came busting in like an Errol Flynn movie." *Jack Kirby at War*, video interview conducted March 17, 1983, filmed by Greg Theakston and Tony Dispoto, posted by The Jack Kirby Museum & Research Center on YouTube.

PAGE 59: "My sergeant hit me on the head with a steel helmet." *Jack Kirby at War*, video interview conducted March 17, 1983, filmed by Greg Theakston and Tony Dispoto, posted by The Jack Kirby Museum & Research Center on YouTube.

PAGE 60 "Jack Kirby on: World War II Influences Part Two," interview conducted by Ray Wyman, Jr. *Jack Kirby Collector #27*, February 2000. P 20.

PAGE 61-62: "Jack Kirby on: World War II Influences Part Two," interview conducted by Ray Wyman, Jr. *Jack Kirby Collector #27*, February 2000. P 20-21.

PAGES 62–63: *Jack Kirby at War*, video interview conducted March 17, 1983, filmed by Greg Theakston and Tony Dispoto, posted by The Jack Kirby Museum & Research Center on YouTube.

PAGE 63: "Then he looked up at each one of them and said, 'What the fuck are these guys doing here?' And he pointed at the map again and yelled, 'What is this? What is this? You're fouling up the whole fucking thing! If you're here, then why the fuck aren't they dead? They are all supposed to be dead.' I myself was saying, 'Well shit on you, I feel great.'" "Jack Kirby on: World War II Influences Part Two," Interview conducted by Ray Wyman, Jr. *Jack Kirby Collector #27*, February 2000.

PAGE 66: "So I pointed my rifle at his direction like this to make a point and I said, 'I'm sorry you feel that way, but my CO says you have to get in the truck.'" "Jack Kirby on: World War II Influences Part Two," interview conducted by Ray Wyman, Jr. *Jack Kirby Collector #27*, February 2000.

PAGE 66: "And this guy shoots the bicyclist. I turned to him and asked, 'What the hell did you do that for?'" "Jack Kirby & Don Rico Discuss WWII, The Mafia, Watergate, & Comic Art," interview by Don Rico. *Jack Kirby Collector #20*, June 1998. Originally published in *Mysticogryfil*, edited by Barry Alfonso.

PAGES 68–69: "Most of these people were Polish; Polish Jews who were working in some of the nearby factories. I don't remember if the place really had a name, it was a smaller camp—not like Auschwitz, but it was horrible just the same." "Jack Kirby On: World War II Influence," interview by Ray Wyman Jr. *Jack Kirby Collector #27*, February 2000. P 21.

PAGES 68–69: "Looking For the Awesome-8. Call to Duty," by Stan Taylor, published posthumously on kirbymuseum.org.

PAGES 68–69: "Jack Kirby On: Storytelling, Man, God & Nazis," interview by Ray Wyman, Jr. *Jack Kirby Collector #26*, edited by John Morrow. P 8–10.

PAGE 70: "Once I got into a game of poker with some paratroopers; it was like going to a party with a bunch of killers." "Jack Kirby on: World War II Influences Part Two." Interview conducted by Ray Wyman, Jr. *Jack Kirby Collector #27*, February 2000.

PAGE 106: "There was a thing I was involved in, The Fly, which got a reaction and because of that I told Stan there might be a hope for superheroes. 'Why don't we try Captain America again' I kept harping on it and Marvel was quiet in those days, like every other office, and then things began to pick up and gain momentum." "There Is Something Stupid In Violence As Violence," by Mark Herbert. *The Comics Journal Library: Jack Kirby*, edited by Milo George. May 2002.

PAGE 113: "Stan didn't know what a mutation was. I was studying that kind of stuff all the time." "I've Never Done Anything Half-Heartedly," by Gary Groth. *The Comics Journal Library: Jack Kirby*, edited by Milo George. May 2002.

PAGE 118: The claim that Jack Kirby may have written the script for *Fantastic Four #6* was put forth by Mike Breen in *The Jack Kirby Collector #61*. His observation was that the scripting in that issue had more in common with Kirby's solo work than with any of the other issues of *Fantastic Four* scripted by Stan Lee. I agree with this assessment. Longtime Marvel editor Tom Brevoort references this article agrees that Jack Kirby wrote the script to issue 6 and goes into detail about it on his blog at Tombrevoort.com. "That Is Strong Talk . . . Whoever You Are" by Mike Breen, *The Jack Kirby Collector #61*. 2013.

PAGES 131-132: Art Vs. Commerce: Kirby's battles with Marvel Comics over original art and copyrights, by John Morrow. *The Jack Kirby Collector #24*. April 1999.

PAGE 136: An Interview with Jim Steranko, by Robin Green. *Rolling Stone* #91, September, 1971.

PAGE 137: "A Failure to Communicate: Part Four" By Mike Gartland. *The Jack Kirby Collector #24*, April 1999. P 12–17.

PAGE 139: "Would You Like To See My Etchings?" Interview with Roz Kirby by John Morrow. *The Collected Jack Kirby Collector Volume Two*, edited by John Morrow. 1998. P 47.

PAGE 152: "The Thin Black Line," by Robert L. Bryant, Jr. *Jack Kirby Collector #28*. April 2000. P 27. "The next day we're up at the Marvel offices, and there are (Jack's) pages pinned all over the doors. Vince Colletta had been xeroxing them and taking them up there." The 1997 Kirby Tribute Panel, featuring Mark Evanier. Transcribed by John Morrow. *The Jack Kirby Collector #17*. November, 1997.

PAGE 155: "Would You Like To See My Etchings?" Interview with Roz Kirby by John Morrow. *The Collected Jack Kirby Collector Volume Two*, edited by John Morrow. 1998. P 50.

PAGE 163: "A Shocking Story" by Nicholas Caputo. *The Collected Jack Kirby Collector Volume Two*, edited by John Morrow. 1998. P 60.

PAGE 174: "Would You Like To See My Etchings?" Interview with Roz Kirby by John Morrow. *The Collected Jack Kirby Collector Volume Two*, edited by John Morrow. 1998. P 50.

PAGE 177: "Would You Like To See My Etchings?" Interview with Roz Kirby by John Morrow. *The Collected Jack Kirby Collector Volume Two*, edited by John Morrow. 1998. P 51.

PAGE 177: "He couldn't even walk into a toy store with his grandson. All the Hulk playthings on display, many of them sporting Jack Kirby drawings, made him physically ill." *Kirby King of Comics* by Mark Evanier. 2008. P 203.

PAGE 182: Jack Kirby's cigar habit resulted in "esophageal cancer later in life." "Hero Complex" by, Neal Kirby, the *Los Angeles Times*. April 9, 2012.

PAGE 183: Roz Kirby: "He put a note in the Wall, so I said to him, 'What did you write?' And he says, 'Thanks for the vacation.'" "Would You Like To See My Etchings?" Interview with Rom Kirby by John Morrow. *The Collected Jack Kirby Collector Volume Two*, edited by John Morrow. 1998. P 44.

PAGE 186: Rob Liefeld tells this story of Jack Kirby saying this on a comic-con panel when asked what advantage a comics artist has over a movie. Liefeld told the story at the Jack Kirby Tribute Panel at San Diego Comic-Con 2015.

PAGE 187: Possibly Jack Kirby's final interview, dated January 20, 1994. Chrissie Harper conducted the interview, asking this question on behalf of Fabio Barbieri. *Jack Kirby Quarterly #15*, 2008.

PAGE 187: February 6, 1994, Jack Kirby dies of congestive heart failure according to *New York Times* obituary.

PAGE 188: Stan Lee was at Jack Kirby's funeral after asking Roz's permission, but "stayed in the back." He was heard to say this quote about the penciler/inker pairing of Jack and Steve. Jordan Raphael and Tom Spurgeon's *Stan Lee and The Rise and Fall of the American Comic Book*.

PAGE 188: Frank Miller was one of many who eulogized Jack Kirby at his funeral, including Glen Danzig. *Jack Kirby Collector #16*. The text here is not from Jack's funeral, but from Frank Miller's keynote speech to Diamond Comic Distributors Retailers Seminar, June 12, 1994, as printed in *Sin City: The Big Fat Kill #5* by Frank Miller.

PAGE 188: When the "Silver Surfer" cartoon first aired, the credits listed Jack Kirby above Stan Lee. Every subsequent airing had the titles reversed.

PAGE 190: "Marvel & Jack Kirby Heirs Settle Legal Battle Ahead Of Supreme Court Showdown'" by Dominic Patten, *Deadline Hollywood News*. September 26, 2014.

BIBLIOGRAPHY

Evanier, Mark. *Kirby: King of Comics*. New York, NY; Abrams, 2008.

Groth, Gary and various. *Jack Kirby: The Comics Journal Library*. Seattle, WA; Fantagraphics Books, 2002.

Hadju, David. *The Ten-Cent Plague*. New York, NY; Picador, 2008.

Howe, Sean. *Marvel Comics: The Untold Story*. New York, NY; Harper, 2012.

Lee, Stan. *Origins of Marvel Comics*. New York, NY; Simon and Schuster, 1974.

Ro, Ronin. *Tales To Astonish: Jack Kirby, Stan Lee and the American Comic Book Revolution*. New York, NY; Bloomsbury, 2004.

Simon, Joe and Jim Simon. *The Comic Book Makers*. New York, NY; Crestwood/II Publications, 1990.

Theakston, Greg. *The Complete Jack Kirby*. Brooklyn, NY; Pure Imagination Publishing, 1997.

Theakston, Greg. *Comic Strip Kirby*. Brooklyn, NY; Pure Imagination Publishing, 2006.

Theakston, Greg. *Jack Magic*. Brooklyn, NY; Pure Imagination Publishing, 2011.

Wyman, Ray. *The Art of Jack Kirby*. Orange, California; The Blue Rose Press, Inc., 1992.

PERIODICALS

Harper, Chrissie, editor. *The Jack Kirby Quarterly*. Brighton, UK; Quality Communications, 1993-2008.

Morrow, John, editor. *The Jack Kirby Collector*. Raleigh, NC; TwoMorrows, 1994-Present.

Thomas, Roy, editor. *Alter Ego #76*. Raleigh, NC; TwoMorrows, 2008.

REFERENCE

FILM/DOCUMENTARIES
Harlan Ellison, "Masters of Comic Art"

WEBSITES
The Jack Kirby Museum & Research Center, https://kirbymuseum.org/

ABOUT THE AUTHOR

GREGORY NEISER

Tom Scioli is a contemporary comics artist who gained prominence as co-creator of *Gødland*, a Kirby-esque space opera which was nominated for an Eisner Award, for Image Comics. He next drew and co-scripted (with IDW editor-in-chief John Barber) *Transformers vs. GI Joe*. Recently, he wrote and drew "Super Powers," a series of short comics appearing in DC's experimental imprint Young Animal. He also recently completed a modern reimagining of *Go-Bots* for IDW. He is known for his unconventional drawing style, dense page layouts, and imaginative writing. He's one of a small number of mainstream comics creators today who writes, draws, colors, and hand-letters his work.

INDEX

All rights reserved.
Published in the United States by Ten Speed Press,
an imprint of Random House, a division of
Penguin Random House LLC, New York.
www.tenspeed.com

Ten Speed Press and the Ten Speed Press colophon are
registered trademarks of Penguin Random House LLC.

Library of Congress Control Number: 2020931843

Hardcover ISBN: 978-1-9848-5690-6
eBook ISBN: 978-1-9848-5691-3

Printed in China.

Design by Chloe Rawlins
Color by Tom Scioli
Color assists by Bill Crabtree

10 9 8 7 6 5 4 3 2 1

First Edition